Crossing the Threshold of Mercy

*A Spiritual Guide for the
Extraordinary Jubilee Year of Mercy*

Edited by Mark-David Janus, CSP, PhD

Paulist Press
New York / Mahwah, NJ

Cover image by Daniel Abel / Photographer
Cover design by Tamian Wood
Book design by Lynn Else

Library of Congress Control Number: 2015946955

ISBN: 978-0-8091-4981-0 (paperback)
ISBN: 978-1-58768-601-6 (e-book)

Published by Paulist Press
997 Macarthur Boulevard
Mahwah, New Jersey 07430

www.paulistpress.com

Printed and bound in the
United States of America

Contents

Contents

Contents

Official Calendar of
Jubilee of Mercy Events

December 2015

Tuesday, December 8, 2015
Solemnity of the Immaculate Conception
Opening of the Holy Door of St. Peter's Basilica

Sunday, December 13, 2015
Third Sunday of Advent
Opening of the Holy Door of the Basilica of St. John
Lateran and in the Cathedrals of the World

January 2016

Friday, January 1, 2016
Solemnity of Mary, the Holy Mother of God
World Day for Peace
Opening of the Holy Door of the Basilica of
Saint Mary Major

Tuesday, January 19–Thursday, January 21, 2016
Jubilee for Those Engaged in Pilgrimage Work

Monday, January 25, 2016
Feast of the Conversion of St. Paul
Opening of the Holy Door of the Basilica of St. Paul
Outside the Walls
"Jubilee" Sign of the Holy Father: Witness of the
Works of Mercy

February 2016

Tuesday, February 2, 2016
Feast of the Presentation of the Lord and the Day for Consecrated Life
Jubilee for Consecrated Life and the closing of the Year for Consecrated Life

Wednesday, February 10, 2016
Ash Wednesday
Sending Forth of the Missionaries of Mercy, St. Peter's Basilica

Monday, February 22, 2016
Feast of the Chair of St. Peter
Jubilee for the Roman Curia
"Jubilee" Sign of the Holy Father: Witness of the Works of Mercy

March 2016

Friday, March 4 and Saturday, March 5, 2016
"Twenty-Four Hours for the Lord" with a Penitential Liturgy in St. Peter's Basilica on the Afternoon of Friday, March 4

Sunday, March 20, 2016
Palm Sunday
The Diocesan Day for Youth in Rome
"Jubilee" Sign of the Holy Father: Witness of the Works of Mercy

April 2016

Sunday, April 3, 2016
Divine Mercy Sunday
Jubilee for Those Who Are Devoted to the
  Spirituality of Divine Mercy

Sunday, April 24, 2016
Fifth Sunday of Easter
Jubilee for Boys and Girls (ages 13–16)
To Profess the Faith and Construct a Culture of Mercy
"Jubilee" Sign of the Holy Father: Witness of the
  Works of Mercy

May 2016

Sunday, May 27–29, 2016
The Solemnity of Corpus Christi in Italy
Jubilee for Deacons

June 2016

Friday, June 3, 2016
Solemnity of the Most Sacred Heart of Jesus
Jubilee for Priests
One Hundred Sixty Years since the Introduction of
  the Feast by Pius IX in 1856

Sunday, June 12, 2016
Eleventh Sunday of Ordinary Time
Jubilee for Those Who Are Ill and for Persons with
  Disabilities
"Jubilee" Sign of the Holy Father: Witness of the
  Works of Mercy

July 2016

Tuesday, July 26–Sunday, July 31, 2016
*To Conclude on the Eighteenth Sunday of
    Ordinary Time*
Jubilee for Young Adults
World Youth Day in Krakow, Poland

September 2016

Sunday, September 4, 2016
Twenty-Third Sunday of Ordinary Time
Memorial of Blessed Teresa of Calcutta (September 5)
Jubilee for Workers and Volunteers of Mercy

Sunday, September 25, 2016
Twenty-Sixth Sunday of Ordinary Time
Jubilee for Catechists

October 2016

Saturday, October 8 and Sunday, October 9, 2016
*Saturday and Sunday after the Memorial of Our Lady
    of the Rosary*
Marian Jubilee

November 2016

Tuesday, November 1, 2016
Solemnity of All Saints
Holy Mass Celebrated by the Holy Father in
    Memory of the Faithful Departed

Sunday, November 6, 2016
Thirty-Second Sunday of Ordinary Time
The Jubilee for Prisoners

Sunday, November 13, 2016
Thirty-Third Sunday of Ordinary Time
Closing of the Holy Doors in the Basilicas of Rome
and in the Dioceses of the World

Sunday, November 20, 2016
*Solemnity of Our Lord Jesus Christ, King of the
Universe*
Closing of the Holy Door of St. Peter's Basilica and
the Conclusion of the Jubilee of Mercy

Introduction

The Church is commissioned to announce the mercy of God,
the beating heart of the gospel, which in its own way
must penetrate the heart and mind of every person.
  ✠Pope Francis[1]

With these words, Pope Francis invites the Church to celebrate
an Extraordinary Jubilee Year of Mercy, which is a pilgrimage, a
journey to the mercy of God. This journey is traditionally sym-
bolized as a pilgrimage to Rome, during which the pilgrim
crosses the threshold of the Holy Doors at the four great basilicas in Rome. Crossing the threshold of the Holy Doors, we cross
the threshold into the mercy of God. Crossing the threshold
means leaving behind doubt and fear and allowing God's love to
embrace us. This pilgrimage is spiritual, not geographic; it represents the journey of our lives, a journey through our self-
understanding, a journey that leads us to a complete and final
trust in the love God is for us. The pilgrimage to the Holy Doors
is a going home for us: "Home is the place that when you have
to go there, they have to take you in. I should have called it
something you somehow haven't to deserve."[2]

    We do not cross the threshold of mercy by ourselves—we
are on pilgrimage with others just as weary, just as failed, just
as frightened and unsure as we. We cannot cross the threshold
of mercy without showing mercy to our fellow pilgrims.
Additionally, crossing the threshold of mercy demands that we
be merciful to those not with us on the journey: those too weak,
too burdened, too depressed, guilty, and ashamed to make the
trip. We must also be aware of all those who do not cross the

threshold of mercy because they do not believe there is anything on the other side, no God to embrace them, no mercy to cover them; those so hardened by life that they have come to see mercy as a weakness to be avoided, not a strength to be welcomed.

A pilgrimage is arduous work inside as well as out, so we offer this book to you as companion and comfort for your pilgrimage to cross the threshold of mercy. We hope that you will draw inspiration from the words of Sacred Scripture, the thoughts of Pope Francis, and the words of those that inspire him. Have an Extraordinary Jubilee Year of Mercy.

Mark-David Janus

Celebrating the Jubilee Year of Mercy

Prayer of Pope Francis for the Jubilee of Mercy

Lord Jesus Christ,
you have taught us to be merciful like the heavenly Father,
and have told us that whoever sees you sees Him.
Show us your face and we will be saved.
Your loving gaze freed Zacchaeus and Matthew from being
*   enslaved by money;*
the adulteress and Magdalene from seeking happiness only in
*   created things;*
made Peter weep after his betrayal,
and assured Paradise to the repentant thief.
Let us hear, as if addressed to each one of us, the words that
*   you spoke to the Samaritan woman:*
"If you knew the gift of God!"

You are the visible face of the invisible Father,
of the God who manifests his power above all by forgiveness
*   and mercy:*
let the Church be your visible face in the world, its Lord risen
*   and glorified.*
You willed that your ministers would also be clothed in
*   weakness*
in order that they may feel compassion for those in ignorance
*   and error:*

*let everyone who approaches them feel sought after, loved, and
    forgiven by God.*

*Send your Spirit and consecrate every one of us with its
    anointing,
so that the Jubilee of Mercy may be a year of grace from the
    Lord,
and your Church, with renewed enthusiasm, may bring good
    news to the poor,
proclaim liberty to captives and the oppressed,
and restore sight to the blind.*

*We ask this through the intercession of Mary, Mother of
    Mercy,
you who live and reign with the Father and the Holy Spirit for
    ever and ever.
Amen.*

DECEMBER 8, 2015: OPENING THE HOLY DOOR AT ST. PETER'S BASILICA, ROME

Mercy is the very foundation of the Church's life. All of her pastoral activity should be caught up in the tenderness she makes present to believers; nothing in her preaching and in her witness to the world can be lacking in mercy. The Church's very credibility is seen in how she shows merciful and compassionate love. The Church "has an endless desire to show mercy." Perhaps we have long since forgotten how to show and live the way of mercy. The temptation, on the one hand, to focus exclusively on justice made us forget that this is only the first, albeit necessary and indispensable step. But the Church needs to go beyond and strive for a higher and more important goal. On the other hand, sad to say, we must admit that the practice of mercy is waning in the wider culture. In some cases the word seems to have dropped out of use. However, without a witness to mercy, life becomes fruitless and sterile, as if sequestered in a barren desert. The time has come for the Church to take up the joyful call to mercy once more. It is time to return to the basics and to bear the weaknesses and struggles of our brothers and sisters. Mercy is the force that reawakens us to new life and instills in us the courage to look to the future with hope.[1]

The practice of *pilgrimage* has a special place in the Holy Year, because it represents the journey each of us makes in this life. Life itself is a pilgrimage, and the human being is a *viator*, a pilgrim traveling along the road, making his way to the desired destination. Similarly, to reach the Holy Door in Rome or in any other place in the world, everyone, each according to his or her ability, will have to make a pilgrimage. This will be a sign that mercy is also a goal to reach and requires dedication and sacrifice. May pilgrimage be an impetus to conversion: by crossing the threshold of the Holy Door, we will find the strength to embrace God's mercy and dedicate ourselves to being merciful with others as the Father has been with us. ✚Pope Francis[2]

The Church is called to be the house of the Father, with doors always wide open. One concrete sign of such openness is that our church doors should always be open, so that if someone, moved by the Spirit, comes there looking for God, he or she will not find a closed door. There are other doors that should not be closed either. Everyone can share in some way in the life of the Church; everyone can be part of the community, nor should the doors of the sacraments be closed for simply any reason. This is especially true of the sacrament which is itself "the door": baptism. The Eucharist, although it is the fullness of sacramental life, is not a prize for the perfect but a powerful medicine and nourishment for the weak. These convictions have pastoral consequences that we are called to consider with prudence and boldness. Frequently, we act as arbiters of grace rather than its facilitators. But the Church is not a tollhouse; it is the house of the Father, where there is a place for everyone, with all their problems. ✠Pope Francis[3]

Advent

Have you not known? Have you not heard?
The LORD is the everlasting God,
the Creator of the ends of the earth.
He does not faint or grow weary;
his understanding is unsearchable.
He gives power to the faint,
and strengthens the powerless.
Even youths will faint and be weary,
and the young will fall exhausted;
but those who wait for the LORD shall renew their strength,
they shall mount up with wings like eagles,
they shall run and not be weary,
they shall walk and not faint.

Isaiah 40:28–31

God is he who comes to save us and who seeks to help, especially those who are fearful of heart. His coming among us strengthens us, makes us steadfast, gives us courage, makes the desert and the steppe rejoice and blossom; that is, when our lives become arid. And when do our lives become arid? When they lack the water of God's Word and his Spirit of love. However great our limitations and dismay, we are not allowed to be sluggish and vacillating when faced with difficulty and our own weakness. On the contrary, we are invited to strengthen the weak hands, to make firm the feeble knees, to be strong and to fear not, because our God always shows us the greatness of his mercy. He gives us the strength to go forward. He is always with us in order to help us to go forward. He is a God who loves us so very much, he loves us and that is why he is with us, to help us, to strengthen us, help us go forward. Courage! Always forward! ✦Pope Francis[1]

God does not wait for us to go to him but it is he who moves toward us, without calculation, without qualification. That is what God is like. He always takes the first step, he comes toward us. ✦Pope Francis[2]

Let us never tire, therefore, of seeking the Lord—*of letting ourselves be sought by Him*—of tending over our relationship with Him in silence and prayerful listening. Let us keep our gaze fixed on Him, the center of time and history; let us make room for His presence within us: He is the principle and foundation of mercy which envelops our weaknesses and transforms and renews everything; He is the most precious thing we are called to offer to our people, who otherwise are left at the mercy of an indifferent society, if not in despair. Every man lives by Him, even if he ignores Him. ✦Pope Francis[3]

Soon afterwards he went to a town called Nain, and his disciples and a large crowd went with him. As he approached the gate of the town, a man who had died was being carried out. He was his mother's only son, and she was a widow; and with her was a large crowd from the town. When the Lord saw her, he had compassion for her and said to her, "Do not weep." Then he came forward

and touched the bier, and the bearers stood still. And he said, "Young man, I say to you, rise!" The dead man sat up and began to speak, and Jesus gave him to his mother. Fear seized all of them; and they glorified God, saying, "A great prophet has risen among us!" and "God has looked favorably on his people!" This word about him spread throughout Judea and all the surrounding country. (Luke 7:11–17)

What is the fruit of this love and mercy? It is life! Jesus says to the widow of Nain: "Do not weep" and then he calls the dead boy and awakes him as if from sleep. Let's think about this, it's beautiful: God's mercy gives life to man, it raises him from the dead. Let us not forget that the Lord always watches over us with mercy; he always watches over us with mercy. Let us not be afraid of approaching him! He has a merciful heart! If we show him our inner wounds, our inner sins, he will always forgive us. It is pure mercy. Let us go to Jesus! ✠Pope Francis[4]

DECEMBER 12, 2015: LADY OF GUADALUPE

When Our Lady appeared to Saint Juan Diego, her face was that of a woman of mixed blood, a *mestiza*, and her garments bore many symbols of the native culture. Like Jesus, Mary is close to all her sons and daughters; as a concerned mother, she accompanies them on their way through life. She shares all the joys and hopes, the sorrows and troubles of God's People, which is made up of men and women of every race and nation.

When the image of the Virgin appeared on the tilma of Juan Diego, it was the prophecy of an embrace: Mary's embrace of all the peoples of the vast expanses of America—the peoples who already lived there, and those who were yet to come. Mary's embrace showed what America—North and South—is called to be: a land where different peoples come together; a land prepared to accept human life at every stage, from the mother's womb to old age; a land which welcomes immigrants, and the poor and the marginalized, in every age. A land of generosity.

That is the message of Our Lady of Guadalupe, and it is also my message, the message of the Church. I ask all the people of the Americas to open wide their arms, like the Virgin, with love and tenderness. ✝Pope Francis[5]

DECEMBER 13, 2015: OPENING THE HOLY DOORS OF ST. JOHN LATERAN AND ALL CATHEDRALS

The precept of mercy applies not only to individual Christians, but also to the church as a whole. As in the case of individual Christians, the command for the church to be merciful is grounded in the being of the church as the body of Christ. The church, therefore, is not a kind of social or charitable agency; as the body of Christ, it is the sacrament of the continuing effective presence of Christ in the world. As such, the church is the sacrament of mercy.

It is this sacrament as the "total Christ," that is, Christ in head and members. Thus the church encounters Christ himself in its own members and in people who are in need of help. The church is supposed to make present the gospel of mercy, which Jesus Christ is in person, through word, sacrament, its whole life in history, and the life of individual Christians.

However, the church too is the object of God's mercy. As the body of Christ, it is redeemed by Jesus Christ. But the church encompasses sinners in its bosom and, therefore, must be purified time and again in order to be able to stand there, pure and holy. Consequently, the church must self critically ask itself repeatedly whether it actually lives up to that which it is and should be. Conversely, just as Jesus Christ did, so too we are supposed to deal with the flaws and failings of the church, not in a self-righteous, but in a merciful way.

We must, however, be clear about one thing: a church without charity and without mercy would no longer be the church of Jesus Christ. ✢Walter Cardinal Kasper[6]

The LORD is merciful and gracious,
slow to anger and abounding in steadfast love.
He will not always accuse,
nor will he keep his anger forever.
He does not deal with us according to our sins,
nor repay us according to our iniquities.
For as the heavens are high above the earth,
so·great is his steadfast love toward those who fear him;
as far as the east is from the west,
so far he removes our transgressions from us.
As a father has compassion for his children,
so the LORD has compassion for those who fear him.
For he knows how we were made;
he remembers that we are dust.

Psalm 103:8–14

In the Bible God always appears as the one who takes the initiative in the encounter with man: it is he who seeks man, and usually he seeks him precisely while man is in the bitter and tragic moment of betraying God and fleeing from him. God does not wait in seeking him: he seeks him out immediately. He is a patient seeker, our Father! He goes before us and he waits for us always. He never tires of waiting for us, he is never far from us, but he has the patience to wait for the best moment to meet each one of us. And when the encounter happens, it is never rushed, because God wants to remain at length with us to sustain us, to console us, to give us his joy. God hastens to meet us, but he never rushes to leave us. He stays with us. As we long for him and desire him, so he too desires to be with us, that we may belong to him, we are his "belonging," we are his creatures. He, too, we can say, thirsts for us, to meet us. Our God is thirsty for us. And this is God's heart. ✛Pope Francis[7]

He is our Clothing. In his love he wraps and holds us. He enfolds us in love. He will never let us go. —Julian of Norwich[8]

What is God's plan? It is to make of us all a single family of his children, in which each person feels that God is close and feels loved by him, as in the Gospel parable, feels the warmth of being God's family. ✛Pope Francis[9]

I sought the LORD, and he answered me,
and delivered me from all my fears.

This poor soul cried, and was heard by the LORD,
and was saved from every trouble.

O taste and see that the LORD is good;
happy are those who take refuge in him.

The LORD is near to the brokenhearted,
and saves the crushed in spirit.

Many are the afflictions of the righteous,
but the LORD rescues them from them all.
He keeps all their bones;
not one of them will be broken.

The LORD redeems the life of his servants;
none of those who take refuge in him will be condemned.
                                    Psalm 34:4, 6, 8, 18–20, 22

What do you think? If a shepherd has a hundred sheep,
and one of them has gone astray, does he not leave the
ninety-nine on the mountains and go in search of the one
that went astray? And if he finds it, truly I tell you, he
rejoices over it more than over the ninety-nine that never
went astray. (Matthew 18:12–13)

Have mercy eternal God, on your little sheep, good shepherd that you are! Do not delay your mercy for the world, for already it almost seems they can no longer survive.—St. Catherine of Siena[10]

Our God is a God who searches....His work is to search: to search and seek out the lost in order to invite them back....God cannot abide losing what is his; thus on Holy Thursday Jesus would pray "that none of those whom thou hast given me may be lost....God has a certain weakness of love for those who are furthest away, who are lost. He goes in search of them. And how does he search? He searches to the very end. Like the shepherd who journeys into the darkness looking for his lost sheep until he finds it" or "like the woman who, when she loses her coin, lights a lamp, sweeps the house and seeks diligently until she finds it." God seeks out the lost because he thinks: "I will not lose this son, he is mine! And I don't want to lose him!" ✠Pope Francis[11]

Come to me, all you that are weary and are carrying heavy burdens, and I will give you rest. Take my yoke upon you, and learn from me; for I am gentle and humble in heart, and you will find rest for your souls. For my yoke is easy, and my burden is light. (Matthew 11:28–30)

To think that God, who is all-powerful and holy, concerns himself with the distressing and self-caused situation of human beings, that God sees the wretchedness of poor and miserable people, that he hears their lament, that he bends down in condescension, that he descends to persons in their need and, despite every human infidelity, concerns himself with them again and again, and that he forgives them and gives them another chance, even though they had deserved just punishment—all of this exceeds normal human experience and expec-

tation; all of this transcends human imagination and thought.
✢ Walter Cardinal Kasper[12]

*While he was at Bethany in the house of Simon the leper,
as he sat at the table, a woman came with an alabaster jar
of very costly ointment of nard, and she broke open the
jar and poured the ointment on his head. But some were
there who said to one another in anger, "Why was the
ointment wasted in this way? For this ointment could
have been sold for more than three hundred denarii, and
the money given to the poor." And they scolded her. But
Jesus said, "Let her alone; why do you trouble her? She
has performed a good service for me. For you always have
the poor with you, and you can show kindness to them
whenever you wish; but you will not always have me. She
has done what she could; she has anointed my body
beforehand for its burial. Truly I tell you, wherever the
good news is proclaimed in the whole world, what she has
done will be told in remembrance of her." (Mark 14:3–9)*

Jesus is the incarnation of the Living God, the one who
brings life amid so many deeds of death, amid sin, selfishness,
and self-absorption. Jesus accepts, loves, uplifts, encourages,
forgives, restores the ability to walk, gives back life. Throughout the Gospels we see how Jesus by his words and actions
brings the transforming life of God. This was the experience of
the woman who anointed the feet of the Lord with ointment:
she felt understood, loved, and she responded by a gesture of

love: she let herself be touched by God's mercy, she obtained forgiveness and she started a new life. ✝Pope Francis[13]

Jesus Christ is the face of the Father's mercy. These words might well sum up the mystery of the Christian faith. Mercy has become living and visible in Jesus of Nazareth, reaching its culmination in him. We need constantly to contemplate the mystery of mercy. It is a wellspring of joy, serenity, and peace. Our salvation depends on it.

Mercy: the word reveals the very mystery of the Most Holy Trinity.

Mercy: the ultimate and supreme act by which God comes to meet us.

Mercy: the fundamental law that dwells in the heart of every person who looks sincerely into the eyes of his brothers and sisters on the path of life.

Mercy: the bridge that connects God and man, opening our hearts to the hope of being loved forever despite our sinfulness. ✝Pope Francis[14]

I maintain that above these two, knowledge and love, is mercy. In the highest and purest that God can work, there is where he works mercy. —Meister Eckhart[15]

In those days Mary set out and went with haste to a Judean town in the hill country, where she entered the house of Zechariah and greeted Elizabeth. (Luke 1:39–40)

16

Regarding this love, regarding this mercy, the divine grace poured into our hearts, one single thing is asked in return: unreserved giving. Not one of us can buy salvation! Salvation is a free gift of the Lord, a free gift of God that comes within us and dwells in us. As we have received freely, so are we called to give freely (cf. Matt 10:8); imitating Mary, who, immediately upon receiving the Angel's announcement, went to share the gift of her fruitfulness with her relative Elizabeth. Because if everything has been given to us, then everything must be passed on. How? By allowing that the Holy Spirit make of us a gift for others. The Spirit is a gift for us and we, by the power of the Spirit, must be a gift for others and allow the Holy Spirit to turn us into instruments of acceptance, instruments of reconciliation, instruments of forgiveness. If our life is allowed to be transformed by the grace of the Lord, for the grace of the Lord does transform us, we will not be able to keep to ourselves the light that comes from his face, but we will let it pass on to enlighten others. ✠Pope Francis[16]

In the sixth month the angel Gabriel was sent by God to a town in Galilee called Nazareth, to a virgin engaged to a man whose name was Joseph, of the house of David. The virgin's name was Mary. And he came to her and said, "Greetings, favored one! The Lord is with you." But she was much perplexed by his words and pondered what sort of greeting this might be. The angel said to her, "Do not be afraid, Mary, for you have found favor with

God. And now, you will conceive in your womb and bear a son, and you will name him Jesus. He will be great, and will be called the Son of the Most High, and the Lord God will give to him the throne of his ancestor David. He will reign over the house of Jacob forever, and of his kingdom there will be no end." Mary said to the angel, "How can this be, since I am a virgin?" The angel said to her, "The Holy Spirit will come upon you, and the power of the Most High will overshadow you; therefore the child to be born will be holy; he will be called Son of God. And now, your relative Elizabeth in her old age has also conceived a son; and this is the sixth month for her who was said to be barren. For nothing will be impossible with God." Then Mary said, "Here am I, the servant of the Lord; let it be with me according to your word." (Luke 1:26–38)

The Word, who found a home in the virgin womb of Mary, comes in the celebration of Christmas to knock once again at the heart of every Christian. He comes and knocks. Each of us is called to respond, like Mary, with a personal and sincere "yes," placing oneself fully at the disposal of God and of his mercy, of his love. ✝Pope Francis[17]

Christmastide

May the Nativity of the Lord, now at hand, rekindle hope and love in your hearts. The birth of the Lord Jesus, which we shall be commemorating in a few days, reminds us of his mission to bring salvation to all men and women, excluding no one. His salvation is not imposed but reaches us through acts of love, mercy, and forgiveness that we ourselves can carry out. The Child of Bethlehem will be happy when all human beings return to God with a renewed heart. Let us ask him in silence and prayer to be all released from the prison of sin, pride, and conceit. In fact, if they are to be truly free from evil, anguish, and death, each and every person needs to come out of this inner prison. Only the Child who was laid in the manger can give complete liberation to all! ✛Pope Benedict XVI[1]

In order to have a complete picture of the reality of that event, in order to penetrate more deeply still into the realism of that moment and the realism of human hearts, let us remember that the event occurred precisely in the way it did: in abandonment and extreme poverty, in the cave stable outside the town, because people in the town refused to receive the Mother and Joseph into any of their homes. Nowhere was there room. From the beginning, the world showed itself inhospitable toward the God who was to be born as Man. Now let us reflect briefly on the lasting meaning of this lack of hospitality on man's part toward God....On this night let us therefore think of all the human beings that fall victim to man's inhumanity, to cruelty, to the lack of any respect, to contempt for the objective rights of every human being. Let us think of those who are lonely, old, or sick; of the homeless, those suffering from hunger, and those whose misery is the result of the exploitation and injustice of economic systems. Let us also think of those who on this night are not allowed to take part in the liturgy of God's Birth and who have no priest to celebrate Mass. And let us give a thought also to those whose souls and consciences are tormented no less than their faith. The stable at Bethlehem is the first place for solidarity with man: for one man's solidarity with another and for all men's with all men, especially with those for whom there is "no room at the inn" (cf. Luke 2:7), whose personal rights are refused recognition. ✝St. Pope John Paul II[2]

This story bursts all normal notions and expectations: the birth of the savior from a virgin, not in a palace, but in the stable of a shelter in the midst of poor, despised shepherds. Something like this is not made up. This is not the language of a saga or myth. At the beginning a stable, at the end the gallows—"this is taken from historical stuff, not the golden stuff beloved of legend." But precisely in this paradox and tension between the heavenly singing of angels and the brutal historical reality, a quite unique magic emanates particularly from the Christmas story, a magic that has always elevated the spirits of many and has touched their hearts....

To this very day, many people, even those who are alienated from the life of the church, visit the divine child in the crib, who is experienced as love's ray of light and hope in a dark and cold world. ✝Walter Cardinal Kasper[3]

In that region there were shepherds living in the fields, keeping watch over their flock by night. Then an angel of the Lord stood before them, and the glory of the Lord shone around them, and they were terrified. But the angel said to them, "Do not be afraid; for see—I am bringing you good news of great joy for all the people: to you is born this day in the city of David a Savior, who is the Messiah, the Lord. This will be a sign for you: you will find a child wrapped in bands of cloth and lying in a manger." And suddenly there was with the angel a multitude of the heavenly host, praising God and saying,

"Glory to God in the highest heaven,
and on earth peace among those whom he favors!"

Luke 2:8–14

When the angels announced the birth of the Redeemer to the shepherds, they did so with these words: "This will be a sign for you: you will find a baby wrapped in swaddling clothes and lying in a manger" (Luke 2:12). The "sign" is in fact the humility of God, the humility of God taken to the extreme; it is the love with which, that night, he assumed our frailty, our suffering, our anxieties, our desires, and our limitations. The message that everyone was expecting, that everyone was searching for in the depths of their souls, was none other than the tenderness of God: God who looks upon us with eyes full of love, who accepts our poverty, God who is in love with our smallness. ✝Pope Francis[4]

While they were there, the time came for her to deliver her child. And she gave birth to her firstborn son and wrapped him in bands of cloth, and laid him in a manger, because there was no place for them in the inn. (Luke 2:6–7)

On this holy night, while we contemplate the Infant Jesus just born and placed in the manger, we are invited to reflect. How do we welcome the tenderness of God? Do I allow myself to be taken up by God, to be embraced by him, or do I prevent him from drawing close? "But I am searching for the Lord"—we could respond. Nevertheless, what is most important is not seeking him, but rather allowing him to seek me, find me, and caress me with tenderness. The question put to us simply by the Infant's presence is: Do I allow God to love me? ✝Pope Francis[5]

In the beginning was the Word, and the Word was with God, and the Word was God. He was in the beginning with God. All things came into being through him, and without him not one thing came into being. What has come into being in him was life, and the life was the light of all people. The light shines in the darkness, and the darkness did not overcome it....

And the Word became flesh and lived among us, and we have seen his glory, the glory as of a father's only son, full of grace and truth....From his fullness we have all received, grace upon grace....No one has ever seen God. It is God the only Son, who is close to the Father's heart, who has made him known. (John 1:1–5, 14, 16, 18)[6]

The grace which was revealed in our world is Jesus, born of the Virgin Mary, true man and true God. He has entered our history; he has shared our journey. He came to free us from darkness and to grant us light. In him was revealed the grace, the mercy, and the tender love of the Father: Jesus is Love incarnate. He is not simply a teacher of wisdom, he is not an ideal for which we strive while knowing that we are hopelessly distant from it. He is the meaning of life and history, who has pitched his tent in our midst. ✢Pope Francis[7]

God has a real face, he has a name: God is mercy, God is faithfulness, he is life which is given to us all. ✢Pope Francis[8]

But when the goodness and loving kindness of God our Savior appeared, he saved us, not because of any works of righteousness that we had done, but according to his mercy, through the water of rebirth and renewal by the Holy Spirit. This Spirit he poured out on us richly through Jesus Christ our Savior, so that, having been justified by his grace, we might become heirs according to the hope of eternal life. (Titus 3:4–7)[9]

God's becoming man is a great mystery! But the reason for all this is his love, a love which is grace, generosity, a desire to draw near, a love which does not hesitate to offer itself in sacrifice for the beloved. Charity, love, is sharing with the one we love in all things. Love makes us similar, it creates equality, it breaks down walls and eliminates distances. God did this with us. Indeed, Jesus "worked with human hands, thought with a human mind, acted by human choice and loved with a human heart." ✝Pope Francis[10]

FEAST OF THE HOLY FAMILY

The Baby Jesus with his Mother Mary and with St. Joseph are a simple but so luminous icon of the family. The light it casts is the light of mercy and salvation for all the world, the light of truth for every man, for the human family, and for individual families. This light which comes from the Holy Family encourages us to offer human warmth in those family situations in which, for various reasons, peace is lacking, harmony is lacking, and forgiveness is lacking. May our concrete solidarity not diminish especially with regard to the families who are experiencing more difficult situations due to illness, unemployment, discrimination, the need to emigrate....Let us pause here for a moment and pray in silence for all these families in difficulty, whether due to problems of illness, unemployment, discrimination, need to emigrate, due to difficulty in understanding each other and also to disunion. Let us pray in silence for all these families. ✝Pope Francis[11]

But the basis of this feeling of deep joy is the presence of God, the presence of God in the family and his love, which is welcoming, merciful, and respectful toward all. And above all, a love which is patient: patience is a virtue of God and he teaches us how to cultivate it in family life, how to be patient, and lovingly so, with each other. ✝Pope Francis[12]

FEAST OF THE HOLY INNOCENTS

Now after they had left, an angel of the Lord appeared to Joseph in a dream and said, "Get up, take the child and his mother, and flee to Egypt, and remain there until I tell you; for Herod is about to search for the child, to destroy him." Then Joseph got up, took the child and his mother by night, and went to Egypt, and remained there until the death of Herod. This was to fulfill what had been spoken by the Lord through the prophet, "Out of Egypt I have called my son." When Herod saw that he had been tricked by the wise men, he was infuriated, and he sent and killed all the children in and around Bethlehem who were two years old or under, according to the time that he had learned from the wise men. Then was fulfilled what had been spoken through the prophet Jeremiah:

"A voice was heard in Ramah,
wailing and loud lamentation,
Rachel weeping for her children;
she refused to be consoled, because they are no more."

Matthew 2:13–18

A much-discussed form of such pseudomercy nowadays consists in protecting the wrongdoer more than the victim. Such indulgence can occur because of misguided friendship or collegiality. It can also happen because one wants to protect an institution—whether it be the church, the state, a religious order, or club—from the adverse consequences of uncovering and prosecuting wrongdoing. Such a mindset goes against the spirit of the gospel, which advances the preferential option for the poor and advocates for whoever is the weaker. Protection of the victim, therefore, must precede protection of the offender. ✝Walter Cardinal Kasper[13]

NEW YEAR'S EVE

As the year draws to a close, we gather up, as in a basket, the days, weeks, and months we have lived in order to offer them all to the Lord. And let us courageously ask ourselves: How have we lived the time which He has given us? Have we used it primarily for ourselves, for our own interests, or have we also sought to spend it on others? ✝Pope Francis[14]

At the dawn of this New Year, we are all called to rekindle in our heart an impulse of hope, which must be translated into concrete works of peace. "Are you in disaccord with this person? Make peace!"; "At home? Make peace!"; "In your community? Make peace!"; "At your place of work? Make peace!" Work for peace, for reconciliation and fraternity. Each of us must perform gestures of fraternity toward our neighbor, especially toward those who are tried by family tensions or various types of conflict. These small gestures are of so much value: they can be seeds which give hope, they can open paths and perspectives of peace. ✝Pope Francis[15]

NEW YEAR'S DAY: OPENING OF THE HOLY DOOR AT ST. MARY MAJOR

Mother, you who know what it means
to clasp in your arms the dead body of your Son,
of him to whom you gave birth,
spare all mothers on this earth the death of their sons,

the torments, the slavery, the destruction of war,
the persecutions, the concentration camps,
the prisons!
Keep for them the joy of birth,
of sustenance, of the development of man and of his life.
In the name of this life,
in the name of the birth of the Lord,
implore with us peace, and justice in the world!
Mother of Peace,
in all the beauty and majesty of your motherhood,
which the Church exalts and the world admires,
we pray to you:
Be with us at every moment!
Let this New Year be a year of peace,
in virtue of the birth and the death of your Son! Amen.

✝St. Pope John Paul II[16]

NEW YEAR'S DAY: WORLD DAY OF PEACE

The theme of this World Day of Peace is "Fraternity, the Foundation and Pathway to Peace."…It is based on the conviction that we are all children of the one Heavenly Father, we belong to the same human family, and we share a common destiny. Hence derives each person's responsibility to work so that the world might become a community of brothers and sisters who respect one another, accept one another in their differences and take care of one another. We are also called to be aware of the violence and injustices which are present in so many parts of the world to which we cannot remain indifferent and unmoved: everyone's commitment is needed in order to build a truly just and caring society. Yesterday I received a letter from a gentleman, perhaps one of you, who, in bringing a family tragedy to my attention, went on to list the many tragedies and wars that exist today in the world, and he asked me: What is happening in the heart of man which is leading him to do such things? And at the end he said: "It is time to stop." I too believe it would do us good to stop on this path of violence and seek peace. Brothers and sisters, I make the words of this man my own: What is happening in the heart of man? What is happening in the heart of humanity? It is time to stop! ✢Pope Francis[17]

> As God's chosen ones, holy and beloved, clothe yourselves with compassion, kindness, humility, meekness, and patience. Bear with one another and, if anyone has a complaint against another, forgive each other; just as the Lord has forgiven you, so you also must forgive. Above all, clothe yourselves with love, which binds everything together in perfect harmony. And let the peace of Christ rule in your hearts, to which indeed you were called in the one body. And be thankful. Let the word of Christ dwell in you richly; teach and admonish one another in all wisdom; and with gratitude in your hearts sing psalms, hymns, and spiritual songs to God. And whatever you do, in word or deed, do everything in the name of the Lord Jesus, giving thanks to God the Father through him. (Colossians 3:12–17)[18]

FEAST OF THE EPIPHANY

> They set out; and there, ahead of them, went the star that they had seen at its rising, until it stopped over the place where the child was. When they saw that the star had stopped, they were overwhelmed with joy. On entering the house, they saw the child with Mary his mother; and

they knelt down and paid him homage. Then, opening their treasure chests, they offered him gifts of gold, frankincense, and myrrh. (Matthew 2:9–11)

Remember well: life is a journey, always a journey, in search of God. Journey attentively, tirelessly, and courageously. And something is missing, one thing is missing: attentively, tirelessly, and courageously…and what is missing? Journey with light! And what is this light? The Gospel, the Word of God. Always with the Gospel: in your pocket, in your purse, in order to read it, always with us. Journey attentively, tirelessly, courageously, and with the light of the Word of God.

To all I wish a happy Feast. Do not forget to pray for me and have a good lunch. *Arrivederci!* ✢Pope Francis[19]

Ordinary Time I

What must we do, Father? Look, read the Beatitudes: that will do you good. If you want to know what you actually have to do, read Matthew Chapter 25, which is the standard by which we will be judged. With these two things you have the action plan: the Beatitudes and Matthew 25. You do not need to read anything else. I ask you this with all my heart. ♰Pope Francis[1]

In proclaiming the Beatitudes, Jesus asks us to follow him and to travel with him along the path of love, the path that alone leads to eternal life. It is not an easy journey, yet the Lord promises us his grace and he never abandons us. We face so many challenges in life: poverty, distress, humiliation, the struggle for justice, persecutions, the difficulty of daily conversion, the effort to remain faithful to our call to holiness, and many others. But if we open the door to Jesus and allow him to be part of our lives, if we share our joys and sorrows with him, then we will experience the peace and joy that only God, who is infinite love, can give. ♰Pope Francis[2]

THE BEATITUDES

When Jesus saw the crowds, he went up the mountain; and after he sat down, his disciples came to him. Then he began to speak, and taught them, saying:

"Blessed are the poor in spirit, for theirs is the kingdom of heaven.

"Blessed are those who mourn, for they will be comforted.

"Blessed are the meek, for they will inherit the earth.

"Blessed are those who hunger and thirst for righteousness, for they will be filled.

"Blessed are the merciful, for they will receive mercy.

"Blessed are the pure in heart, for they will see God.

"Blessed are the peacemakers, for they will be called children of God.

"Blessed are those who are persecuted for righteousness' sake, for theirs is the kingdom of heaven.

"Blessed are you when people revile you and persecute you and utter all kinds of evil against you falsely on my account. Rejoice and be glad, for your reward is great in heaven, for in the same way they persecuted the prophets who were before you." (Matthew 5:1–12)

Dear friends, let these words of Jesus resound in our hearts: "Blessed are the peacemakers, for they shall be called sons of God" (Matt 5:9). Let us ask sincerely for forgiveness for all the times in which we have caused division or misunderstanding within our communities, knowing well that communion is not achieved except through constant conversion. What is conversion? It is asking the Lord for the grace not to speak ill, not to criticize, not to gossip, to love everyone. It is a grace which the Lord gives us. This is what it means to convert the heart. And let us ask that the daily fabric of our relationships may become an ever more beautiful and joyous reflection of the relationship between Jesus and the Father. ✠Pope Francis[3]

Do not the words of the Sermon on the Mount: "Blessed are the merciful, for they shall obtain mercy," constitute, in a certain sense, a synthesis of the whole of the Good News? ✛St. John Paul II[4]

In the name of Jesus Christ crucified and risen, in the spirit of His messianic mission, enduring in the history of humanity, we raise our voices and pray that the Love which is in the Father may once again be revealed at this stage of history, and that, through the work of the Son and Holy Spirit, it may be shown to be present in our modern world and to be more powerful than evil: more powerful than sin and death. We pray for this through the intercession of her who does not cease to proclaim "mercy... from generation to generation," and also through the intercession of those for whom there have been completely fulfilled the words of the Sermon on the Mount: "Blessed are the merciful, for they shall obtain mercy." ✛St. John Paul II[5]

THE LAST JUDGMENT

When the Son of Man comes in his glory, and all the angels with him, then he will sit on the throne of his glory. All the nations will be gathered before him, and he will separate people one from another as a shepherd separates the sheep from the goats, and he will put the sheep at his right hand and the goats at the left. Then the king will say to those at his right hand, "Come, you that are blessed by my Father, inherit the kingdom prepared for you from the foundation of the world; for I was hungry and you gave me food, I was thirsty and you gave me something to drink, I was a stranger and you welcomed me, I was naked and you gave me clothing, I was sick and you took care of me, I was in prison and you visited me." Then the righteous will answer him, "Lord, when was it that we saw you hungry and gave you food, or thirsty and gave you something to drink? And when was it that we saw you a stranger and welcomed you, or naked and gave you clothing? And when was it that we saw you sick or in prison and visited you?" And the king will answer them, "Truly I tell you, just as you did it to one of the least of these who are members of my family, you did it to me." Then he will say to those at his left hand, "You that are accursed, depart from me into the eternal fire prepared for the devil and his angels; for I was hungry and you gave me no food, I was thirsty and you gave me nothing to drink, I was a stranger and you did not welcome me, naked and you did not give me clothing, sick and in prison and you did not visit me." Then they also will answer, "Lord, when was it that we saw you hungry or thirsty or a stranger or naked or sick or in prison, and did not take care of you?" Then he will answer them, "Truly I tell you, just as you did not do it to one of the least of these, you did not do it to me." And these will go away into eternal punishment, but the righteous into eternal life. (Matthew 25:31–46)

The enumeration of the works of love in his great speech about the Last Judgment especially conforms to this Jewish tradition: feed the hungry, give drink to the thirsty, provide shelter for the homeless, clothe the naked, and visit the sick and those in prison (Matt 25:35–39, 42–44). What is striking in this list is that, as the criterion for judgment, Jesus exclusively names works of charity rather than pious deeds. In doing this, Jesus seizes upon the words of the prophet Hosea: "I desire mercy, not sacrifice" (Matt 9:13; 12:7; cf. Hosea 6:6; Sir 35:3). ✝Walter Cardinal Kasper[6]

I ask the Lord for the grace that our heart may be simple, bright with the truth he gives us, and in this way we can be kind, forgiving, understanding with others, big hearted with people, merciful. ✝Pope Francis[7]

Christians are those who let God clothe them with goodness and mercy, with Christ, so as to become, like Christ, servants of God and others. ✝Pope Francis[8]

We cannot escape the Lord's words to us, and they will serve as the criteria upon which we will be judged: whether we have fed the hungry and given drink to the thirsty, welcomed the stranger and clothed the naked, or spent time with the sick and those in prison (cf. Matt 25:31–45). Moreover, we will be asked if we have helped others to escape the doubt that causes them to fall into despair and which is often a source of loneliness; if we have helped to overcome the ignorance in which millions of people live, especially children deprived of the necessary means to free them from the bonds of poverty; if we have been close to the lonely and afflicted; if we have forgiven those who have offended us and have rejected all forms of anger and hate that lead to violence; if we have had the kind of patience God shows, who is so patient with us; and if we have commended our brothers and sisters to the Lord in prayer. ✢Pope Francis[9]

JANUARY 19, 2016: JUBILEE FOR CLERGY, RELIGIOUS, AND LAY FAITHFUL

Thus, in the image of the Good Shepherd, the priest is a man of mercy and compassion, close to his people and a servant to all.

Today we can think of the Church as a "field hospital." Excuse me but I repeat it, because this is how I see it, how I feel it is: a "field hospital." Wounds need to be treated, so many wounds! So many wounds! There are so many people who are wounded by material problems, by scandals, also in the Church….People wounded by the world's illusions….We priests must be there, close to these people. Mercy first means treating the wounds. When someone is wounded, he needs this immediately, not tests such as the level of cholesterol and one's glycemic index….But there's a wound, treat the wound, and then we can look at the results of the tests. Then specialized treatments can be done, but first we need to treat the open wounds. I think this is what is most important at this time. And there are also hidden wounds, because there are people who distance themselves in order to avoid showing their wounds closer….The custom comes to mind, in the Mosaic Law, of the lepers in Jesus' time, who were always kept at a distance in order not to spread the contagion….There are people who distance themselves through shame, through shame, so as not to let their wounds be seen….And perhaps they distance themselves with some bitterness against the Church, but deep down inside there is a wound….They want a caress! And you, dear brothers—I ask you—do you know the wounds of your parishioners? Do you perceive them? Are you close to them? It's the only question. ✢Pope Francis[10]

For you, as men and women consecrated to God, this joy is rooted in the mystery of the Father's mercy revealed in Christ's sacrifice on the cross. Whether the charism of your Institute is directed more to contemplation or to the active life, you are challenged to become "experts" in divine mercy precisely through your life in community. From experience I know that community life is not always easy, but it is a providential training ground for the heart. It is unrealistic not to expect conflicts; misunderstandings will arise and they must be faced. Despite such difficulties, it is in community life that we are called to grow in mercy, forbearance, and perfect charity.

The experience of God's mercy, nourished by prayer and community, must shape all that you are, all that you do. Your chastity, poverty, and obedience will be a joyful witness to God's love in the measure that you stand firmly on the rock of his mercy. That is the rock. This is certainly the case with religious obedience. Mature and generous obedience requires that you cling in prayer to Christ who, taking the form of a servant, learned obedience through what he suffered (cf. *Perfectae Caritatis*, 14). There are no shortcuts: God desires our hearts completely and this means we have to "let go" and "go out" of ourselves more and more.

A lively experience of the Lord's steadfast mercy also sustains the desire to achieve that perfection of charity which is born of purity of heart. Chastity expresses your single-minded dedication to the love of God who is "the strength of our hearts." We all know what a personal and demanding commitment this entails. Temptations in this area call for humble trust in God, vigilance, perseverance, and opening our heart to that wise brother or sister whom the Lord puts on our path. ✝Pope Francis[11]

JANUARY 25, 2016: OPENING OF THE HOLY DOOR OF ST. PAUL OUTSIDE THE WALLS

If I speak in the tongues of mortals and of angels, but do not have love, I am a noisy gong or a clanging cymbal. And if I have prophetic powers, and understand all mysteries and all knowledge, and if I have all faith, so as to remove mountains, but do not have love, I am nothing. If I give away all my possessions, and if I hand over my body so that I may boast, but do not have love, I gain nothing.

Love is patient; love is kind; love is not envious or boastful or arrogant or rude. It does not insist on its own way; it is not irritable or resentful; it does not rejoice in wrongdoing, but rejoices in the truth. It bears all things, believes all things, hopes all things, endures all things.

Love never ends. But as for prophecies, they will come to an end; as for tongues, they will cease; as for knowledge, it will come to an end. For we know only in part, and we prophesy only in part; but when the complete comes, the partial will come to an end. When I was a child, I spoke like a child, I thought like a child, I reasoned like a child; when I became an adult, I put an end to childish ways. For now we see in a mirror, dimly, but then we will see face to face. Now I know only in part; then I will know fully, even as I have been fully known. And now faith, hope, and love abide, these three; and the greatest of these is love. (1 Corinthians 13)

Blessed be the God and Father of our Lord Jesus Christ, the Father of mercies and the God of all consolation, who consoles us in all our affliction, so that we may be able to console those who are in any affliction with the consolation with which we ourselves are consoled by God. For just as the sufferings of Christ are abundant for us, so also our consolation is abundant through Christ. If we are being afflicted, it is for your consolation and salvation; if we are being consoled, it is for your consolation, which you experience when you patiently endure the same sufferings that we are also suffering. Our hope for you is unshaken; for we know that as you share in our sufferings, so also you share in our consolation. (2 Corinthians 1:3–7)

Who will bring any charge against God's elect? It is God who justifies. Who is to condemn? It is Christ Jesus, who died, yes, who was raised, who is at the right hand of God, who indeed intercedes for us. Who will separate us from the love of Christ? Will hardship, or distress, or persecution, or famine, or nakedness, or peril, or sword? As it is written,

> *"For your sake we are being killed all day long;*
>   *we are accounted as sheep to be slaughtered."*

No, in all these things we are more than conquerors through him who loved us. For I am convinced that neither death, nor life, nor angels, nor rulers, nor things present, nor things to come, nor powers, nor height, nor depth, nor anything else in all creation, will be able to separate us from the love of God in Christ Jesus our Lord. (Romans 8:33–39)

Against enthusiastic exuberance, Paul wants to introduce love—the one thing necessary—as a corrective. Without love, everything else—prophecy, understanding mysteries, knowledge, faith, even great works and deeds of charity—is nothing; each is worthless and without fruit. That is also true of the most rhetorically polished sermon, the most learned theology, and the most zealous commitment to orthodox faith, if it is self-righteous, dogmatic, haughty, and lacking in love. Even martyrdom as such doesn't count. Heretics, communists, and others have their martyrs too. Love alone is the distinctive characteristic of the true Christian. "If I…do not have love, I am nothing"

Paul's description of love's way is anything but sentimental. It is very concrete and realistic. Jesus Christ has shown us the way of love. The path by which Jesus descended to us is the only one by which we can ascend to him. In the end, everything else will pass away; only love will remain. Love is the greatest of all things. If only love remains, then too the works of love will remain. They are all that will be at hand at the time of eschatological judgment and they are all that we, so to speak, can produce in the face of judgment. ✠Walter Cardinal Kasper[12]

FEBRUARY 2, 2016: FEAST OF THE PRESENTATION OF THE LORD AND DAY FOR CONSECRATED LIFE

Every consecrated person is a gift for the People of God on its journey. There is a great need for their presence, which strengthens and renews commitment to: spreading the Gospel, Christian education, love for the needy, contemplative prayer;

commitment to human formation, the spiritual formation of young people, and families; commitment to justice and peace in the human family. But let us think a little about what would happen if there were no sisters in hospitals, no sisters in missions, no sisters in schools. Think about a Church without sisters! It is unthinkable: they are this gift, this leaven that carries forward the People of God. These women who consecrate their life to God, who carry forward Jesus' message, are great. ✠Pope Francis[13]

The Church and the world need this testimony of the love and mercy of God. The consecrated, men and women religious, are the testimony that God is good and merciful. Thus it is necessary to appreciate with gratitude the experiences of consecrated life and to deepen our understanding of the different charisms and spiritualities. Prayer is needed so that many young people may answer "yes" to the Lord who is calling them to consecrate themselves totally to him for selfless service to their brothers and sisters; to consecrate one's life in order to serve God and the brethren. ✠Pope Francis[14]

Once again, we have to ask ourselves: Is Jesus really our first and only love, as we promised he would be when we professed our vows? Only if he is, will we be empowered to love, in truth and mercy, every person who crosses our path. For we will have learned from Jesus the meaning and practice of love. We will be able to love because we have his own heart. ✠Pope Francis[15]

Our founders and foundresses shared in Jesus' own compassion when he saw the crowds who were like sheep without a shepherd. Like Jesus, who compassionately spoke his gracious word, healed the sick, gave bread to the hungry and offered his own life in sacrifice, so our founders and foundresses sought in different ways to be the service of all those to whom the Spirit sent them. They did so by their prayers of intercession, their preaching of the Gospel, their works of catechesis, education, their service to the poor and the infirm....The creativity of charity is boundless; it is able to find countless new ways of bringing the newness of the Gospel to every culture and every corner of society.

In a polarized society, where different cultures experience difficulty in living alongside one another, where the powerless encounter oppression, where inequality abounds, we are called to offer a concrete model of community which, by acknowledging the dignity of each person and sharing our respective gifts, makes it possible to live as brothers and sisters. ✝Pope Francis[16]

Lent

ASH WEDNESDAY

Yet even now, says the LORD,
return to me with all your heart,
with fasting, with weeping, and with mourning;
rend your hearts and not your clothing.
Return to the LORD, your God,
for he is gracious and merciful,
slow to anger, and abounding in steadfast love,
and relents from punishing.

Joel 2:12–13

Salvation enters the heart only when we open the heart in the truth of our sins…recognition of sins, our misery, the recognition of what we are and what we are capable of doing or have done is the door that opens to the caress of Jesus, to the forgiveness of Jesus, to the Word of Jesus: Go in peace, your faith has saved you, because you have been brave, you have been courageous in opening your heart to him who alone can save you. ✠Pope Francis[1]

Have mercy on me, O God,
according to your steadfast love;
according to your abundant mercy
blot out my transgressions.
Wash me thoroughly from my iniquity,
and cleanse me from my sin.

For I know my transgressions,
and my sin is ever before me.
Against you, you alone, have I sinned,
and done what is evil in your sight,
so that you are justified in your sentence
and blameless when you pass judgement.
Indeed, I was born guilty,
a sinner when my mother conceived me.

You desire truth in the inward being;
therefore teach me wisdom in my secret heart.
Purge me with hyssop, and I shall be clean;
wash me, and I shall be whiter than snow.
Let me hear joy and gladness;
let the bones that you have crushed rejoice.
Hide your face from my sins,
and blot out all my iniquities.

Create in me a clean heart, O God,
and put a new and right spirit within me.
Do not cast me away from your presence,
and do not take your holy spirit from me.
Restore to me the joy of your salvation,
and sustain in me a willing spirit.

Psalm 51:1–12

Then Peter came and said to him, "Lord, if another member of the church sins against me, how often should I forgive? As many as seven times?" Jesus said to him, "Not seven times, but, I tell you, seventy-seven times." (Matthew 18:21–22)

"First of all, God always forgives! He never tires of forgiving. It is we who tire of asking forgiveness. But He never tires of forgiving." Indeed, "when Peter asks Jesus: How often shall I forgive, seven times?" he received an eloquent reply: "not seven times, but seventy times seven." In other words, "always," because "this is how God forgives: always…if you have lived a life of many sins, many bad things, but at the end, contritely ask for forgiveness, He forgives you straight away. He always forgives."…

"There is another thing God does when He forgives: He celebrates."…

"If one of us goes to the Lord" and says: "Do you remember, in that year I did something bad?" He answers: "No, no, no. I don't remember." Because "once He forgives He no longer remembers, He forgets," while "so often, with others, we 'keep a record': this one did this, another one once did that.…" But God doesn't do this: "He forgives and forgets."…If He forgets, who am I to remember the sins of others? ✝Pope Francis[2]

After this he went out and saw a tax collector named Levi, sitting at the tax booth; and he said to him, "Follow me." And he got up, left everything, and followed him. Then Levi gave a great banquet for him in his house; and

there was a large crowd of tax collectors and others sitting at the table with them. The Pharisees and their scribes were complaining to his disciples, saying, "Why do you eat and drink with tax collectors and sinners?" Jesus answered, "Those who are well have no need of a physician, but those who are sick; I have come to call not the righteous but sinners to repentance." (Luke 5:27–32)

I often visited the Church of St. Louis of France, and I went there to contemplate the painting of "The Calling of St. Matthew" by Caravaggio. That finger of Jesus, pointing at Matthew. That's me. I feel like him. Like Matthew. It is the gesture of Matthew that strikes me: he holds on to his money as if to say, "No, not me! No, this money is mine." Here, this is me, a sinner on whom the Lord has turned his gaze. And this is what I said when they asked me if I would accept my election as pontiff. I am a sinner, but I trust in the infinite mercy and patience of our Lord Jesus Christ, and I accept in a spirit of penance. ✝Pope Francis[3]

Lent is a favorable time for letting Christ serve us so that we in turn may become more like him. This happens whenever we hear the word of God and receive the sacraments, especially the Eucharist. There we become what we receive: the Body of Christ. In this body there is no room for the indifference which so often seems to possess our hearts. ✝Pope Francis[4]

Lent is a fitting time for self-denial; we would do well to ask ourselves what we can give up in order to help and enrich others by our own poverty. Let us not forget that real poverty hurts: no self-denial is real without this dimension of penance. I distrust a charity that costs nothing and does not hurt. ✝Pope Francis[5]

Lent comes to us as a providential time to change course, to recover the ability to react to the reality of evil which always challenges us. Lent is to be lived as a time of conversion, as a time of renewal for individuals and communities, by drawing close to God and by trustfully adhering to the Gospel. In this way, it also allows us to look with new eyes at our brothers and sisters and their needs. That is why Lent is a favorable time to convert to the love of God and neighbor; a love that knows how to make its own the Lord's attitude of gratuitousness and mercy. ✝Pope Francis[6]

You shall not hate in your heart anyone of your kin; you shall reprove your neighbor, or you will incur guilt yourself. You shall not take vengeance or bear a grudge against any of your people, but you shall love your neighbor as yourself: I am the LORD. (Leviticus 19:17–19)

If in our heart there is no mercy, no joy of forgiveness, we are not in communion with God, even if we observe all of his precepts, for it is love that saves, not the practice of precepts alone.

I now ask of you one thing. In silence, let's all think...everyone think of a person with whom we are annoyed, with whom we are angry, someone we do not like. Let us think of that person and in silence, at this moment, let us pray for this person and let us become merciful with this person. ♰Pope Francis[7]

Where do we get if there is no pardon and no forgiveness, when we repay every wrong done to us with a new wrong, taking an eye for an eye, and a tooth for a tooth? After the horrific experience of twentieth-century atrocities, the problem of forgiveness and love of enemy has acquired a sad new currency and, in broad sectors, has led to an urgently needed rethinking. It has become clear that, however much mercy, forgiveness, and pardon are superhuman acts, they are nonetheless highly sensible acts. Only if we extend our hands anew across old ditches that divide, and ask for forgiveness as well as grant forgiveness, can bloody and traumatic conflicts be handled; a process of healing for the injuries that have been suffered be introduced; and the spiral of violence and counterviolence—as well as the vicious circle of guilt and revenge (blood feuds)—be broken. One cannot simply forget the wrong that has been done; still less is one permitted to simply try to sweep it under the table. One must honestly face up to the wrong that he or she has done and admit it. When that happens, it can lead to a reconciled recollection, in which relationships are detoxified and lose their inimical quality. By means of a reconciled memory that heals the wounds of the past, a new beginning can be made and a new, common future becomes possible. ♰Walter Cardinal Kasper[8]

Living our Baptism to the full—the second invitation—also means *not accustoming ourselves to the situations of degradation and misery* that we encounter as we walk along the streets of our cities and towns. There is a risk of passively accepting certain forms of behavior and of not being shocked by the sad reality surrounding us. We become accustomed to violence, as though it were a predictable part of the daily news. We become accustomed to brothers and sisters sleeping on the streets, who have no roof to shelter them. We become accustomed to refugees seeking freedom and dignity, who are not received as they ought to be. We become accustomed to living in a society which thinks it can do without God, in which parents no longer teach their children to pray or to make the sign of the Cross. ✝Pope Francis[9]

You created us out of nothing. So, now that we exist, be merciful and remake the vessels you created and formed in your image and likeness; re-form them to grace in the mercy and blood of your Son. —St. Catherine of Siena[10]

But if the wicked turn away from all their sins that they have committed and keep all my statutes and do what is lawful and right, they shall surely live; they shall not die. None of the transgressions that they have committed shall be remembered against them; for the righteousness that they have done they shall live. Have I any pleasure in the death of the wicked, says the Lord GOD, and not rather that they should turn from their ways and live?...Again, when the wicked turn away from the wickedness they have committed and do what is lawful and right, they shall save their life.

Because they considered and turned away from all the transgressions that they had committed, they shall surely live; they shall not die. (Ezekiel 18:21–23, 27–28)

May the message of mercy reach everyone, and may no one be indifferent to the call to experience mercy. I direct this invitation to conversion even more fervently to those whose behavior distances them from the grace of God. I particularly have in mind men and women belonging to criminal organizations of any kind. For their own good, I beg them to change their lives. The same invitation is extended to those who either perpetrate or participate in corruption. ☩Pope Francis[11]

The Church is commissioned to announce the mercy of God, the beating heart of the Gospel, which in its own way must penetrate the heart and mind of every person. The Spouse of Christ must pattern her behavior after the Son of God who went out to everyone without exception. In the present day, as the Church is charged with the task of the new evangelization, the theme of mercy needs to be proposed again and again with new enthusiasm and renewed pastoral action. It is absolutely essential for the Church and for the credibility of her message that she herself live and testify to mercy. Her language and her gestures must transmit mercy, so as to touch the hearts of all people and inspire them once more to find the road that leads to the Father.

Wherever there are Christians, everyone should find an oasis of mercy. ☩Pope Francis[12]

A mother knows what's important for a child to enable him to walk the right way through life. Moreover she did not learn it from books but from her own heart. The university of mothers is their heart! They learn there how to bring up their children.

This is how the Church is. She is a merciful mother who understands, who has always sought to help and encourage even those of her children who have erred or are erring; she never closes the door to home. She does not judge but offers God's forgiveness, she offers his love which invites even those of her children who have fallen into a deep abyss to continue on their way. The Church is not afraid to enter their darkness to give them hope; nor is the Church afraid to enter our darkness when we are in the dark night of our soul and our conscience to give us hope! Because the Church is mother! ✝Pope Francis[13]

The Lord wants us to belong to a Church that knows how to open her arms and welcome everyone, that is not a house for the few, but a house for everyone, where all can be renewed, transformed, sanctified by his love, the strongest and the weakest, sinners, the indifferent, those who feel discouraged or lost. ✝Pope Francis[14]

Incline your ear, O LORD, and answer me,
for I am poor and needy.

Preserve my life, for I am devoted to you;
save your servant who trusts in you.
You are my God; be gracious to me, O Lord,
for to you do I cry all day long.
Gladden the soul of your servant,
for to you, O Lord, I lift up my soul.
For you, O Lord, are good and forgiving,
abounding in steadfast love to all who call on you.
Give ear, O LORD, to my prayer;
listen to my cry of supplication.
In the day of my trouble I call on you,
for you will answer me.

Teach me your way, O LORD,
that I may walk in your truth;
give me an undivided heart to revere your name.
I give thanks to you, O Lord my God, with my whole heart,
and I will glorify your name forever.
For great is your steadfast love toward me;
you have delivered my soul from the depths of Sheol.

But you, O Lord, are a God merciful and gracious,
slow to anger and abounding in steadfast love and
    faithfulness.
Turn to me and be gracious to me;
give your strength to your servant;
save the child of your serving girl.
Show me a sign of your favor,
so that those who hate me may see it and be put to shame,
because you, LORD, have helped me and comforted me.

Psalm 86:1–7, 11–13, 15–17

FEBRUARY 22, 2016: FEAST OF THE CHAIR OF ST. PETER, JUBILEE FOR THE ROMAN CURIA

Dear brothers!

I read once that priests are like planes: they only make news when they crash, even though so many of them are in the air. Many people criticize, and few pray for them. It is a very touching, but also very true saying, because it points to the importance and the frailty of our priestly service, and how much evil a single priest who "crashes" can do to the whole body of the Church.

Therefore, so as not to fall in these days when we are preparing ourselves for Confession, let us ask the Virgin Mary, Mother of God and Mother of the Church, to heal the wounds of sin which each of us bears in his heart, and to sustain the Church and the Curia so that they can be healthy and health-giving; holy and sanctifying, to the glory of her Son and for our salvation and that of the entire world. Let us ask her to make us love the Church as Christ, her Son and our Lord, loves her, to have the courage to acknowledge that we are sinners in need of his mercy, and not to fear surrendering our hands into her maternal hands. ✠Pope Francis[15]

As the sun was setting, all those who had any who were sick with various kinds of diseases brought them to him; and he laid his hands on each of them and cured them. (Luke 4:40)

God gets involved with our misery, he draws close to our wounds and he heals them with his hands; he became man in order to have hands with which to heal us...God does not save us merely by decree or by law; he saves us with tenderness, he saves us with caresses, he saves us with his life given for us. ✠Pope Francis[16]

We...despite our resolve to follow the Lord Jesus, experience everyday the selfishness and hardness of our heart. When however we recognize ourselves as sinners, God fills us with His mercy and with His love. And He forgives us, He always forgives us. And it is precisely this that makes us grow as God's people, as the Church: not our cleverness, not our merits—we are a small thing, it's not that—but the daily experience of how much the Lord wishes us well and takes care of us. It is this that makes us feel that we are truly His, in His hands, and makes us grow in communion with Him and with one another. ✠Pope Francis[17]

PREPARATION FOR TWENTY-FOUR HOURS FOR THE LORD: REFLECTIONS FOR PENITENTS

Dear brothers and sisters, let us be enveloped by the mercy of God; let us trust in his patience, which always gives us more time. Let us find the courage to return to his house, to dwell in his loving wounds, allowing ourselves to be loved by him and to encounter his mercy in the sacraments. We will feel his wonderful tenderness, we will feel his embrace, and we too will become more capable of mercy, patience, forgiveness, and love. ✠Pope Francis[18]

Let us place the Sacrament of Reconciliation at the center once more in such a way that it will enable people to touch the grandeur of God's mercy with their own hands. For every penitent, it will be a source of true interior peace. ✢Pope Francis[19]

Nowhere else do we encounter the mercy of God so immediately, so directly, and so concretely as when we are told in the name of Jesus: "Your sins are forgiven!" Certainly no one finds it easy to humbly confess his or her sins and, often enough, to confess the same sins over and over again. But everyone who does that and then is told "I absolve you," not generally and anonymously, but concretely and personally, knows of the inner freedom, inner peace, and joy, which this sacrament bestows. It is necessary to discover this sacrament again. That is especially true for priests. For the commission to remit sins is the commission the risen Lord gave to the apostles. It is for every priest, therefore, a duty and a work of mercy to be ready to administer this sacrament. ✢Walter Cardinal Kasper[20]

Come now, let us argue it out,
says the LORD:
though your sins are like scarlet,
they shall be like snow;
though they are red like crimson,
they shall become like wool.

Isaiah 1:18

A little mercy makes the world less cold and more just. We need to understand properly this mercy of God, this merciful Father who is so patient….Let us remember the Prophet Isaiah who says that even if our sins were scarlet, God's love would make them white as snow. This mercy is beautiful! ✠Pope Francis[21]

O eternal Father, your servants are calling to you for mercy. Answer them then. I know you cannot resist giving it to whoever asks you for it. —St. Catherine of Siena[22]

Let us accustom ourselves to deal with God as with our most affectionate and dear friend who loves us more than anybody else. My God! Why is it that scrupulous and anxious souls treat you as if you were a tyrant who demands nothing more from your subjects than fear and trepidation? The result is that they think that God gets angry at every thought that passes through their minds and at every word that slips involuntarily from their lips and wishes to cast them into hell. No! God does not deprive us of his grace. —St. Alphonsus Ligouri[23]

My mercy is comparably greater than all the sins anyone could commit. Thus it displeases me greatly when they consider their sins to be greater, and this is that sin which is not forgiven here or hereafter. Because despair displeases me so much it is my will that they should put their trust in my mercy even at the point of death, after they have spent a life in wickedness. —St. Catherine of Siena[24]

Still today some say: "Christ yes, the Church no." Like those who say "I believe in God but not in priests." But it is the Church herself which brings Christ to us and which brings us to God. The Church is the great family of God's children. Of course, she also has human aspects. In those who make up the Church, pastors and faithful, there are shortcomings, imperfections and sins. The Pope has these too—and many of them; but what is beautiful is that when we realize we are sinners we encounter the mercy of God who always forgives. Never forget it: God always pardons and receives us into his love of forgiveness and mercy. Some people say that sin is an offense to God, but also an opportunity to humble oneself so as to realize that there is something else more beautiful: God's mercy. Let us think about this. ✝Pope Francis[25]

In this sense, the day of our Baptism is the point of departure for this most beautiful journey, a journey toward God that lasts a lifetime, a journey of conversion that is continually sustained by the Sacrament of Penance. Think about this: when we go to confess our weaknesses, our sins, we go to ask the pardon of Jesus, but we also go to renew our Baptism through his forgiveness. And this is beautiful, it is like celebrating the day of Baptism in every Confession.

In the Sacrament of Baptism all sins are remitted, original sin and all of our personal sins, as well as the suffering of sin. With Baptism the door to an effectively new life is opened, one which is not burdened by the weight of a negative past, but rather already feels the beauty and the goodness of the Kingdom of Heaven. It is the powerful intervention of God's mercy in our lives, to save us. This saving intervention does not take away our human nature and its weakness—we are all weak and we are all sinners—and it does not take from us our responsibility to ask for forgiveness every time we err!

I cannot be baptized many times, but I can go to Confession and by doing so renew the grace of Baptism. It is as though I were being baptized for a second time. The Lord Jesus is very very good and never tires of forgiving us. Even when the door that Baptism opens to us in order to enter the Church is a little closed, due to our weaknesses and our sins. Confession reopens it, precisely because it is a second Baptism that forgives us of everything and illuminates us to go forward with the light of the Lord. ✚Pope Francis[26]

Then Jesus said, "There was a man who had two sons. The younger of them said to his father, 'Father, give me the share of the property that will belong to me.' So he divided his property between them. A few days later the younger son gathered all he had and traveled to a distant country, and there he squandered his property in dissolute living. When he had spent everything, a severe famine took place throughout that country, and he began to be in need. So he went and hired himself out to one of the citizens of that country, who sent him to his fields to feed the pigs. He would gladly have filled himself with the pods that the pigs were eating; and no one gave him anything. But when he came to himself he said, 'How many of my father's hired hands have bread enough and to spare, but

here I am dying of hunger! I will get up and go to my father, and I will say to him, "Father, I have sinned against heaven and before you; I am no longer worthy to be called your son; treat me like one of your hired hands."' So he set off and went to his father. But while he was still far off, his father saw him and was filled with compassion; he ran and put his arms around him and kissed him. Then the son said to him, 'Father, I have sinned against heaven and before you; I am no longer worthy to be called your son.' But the father said to his slaves, 'Quickly, bring out a robe—the best one—and put it on him; put a ring on his finger and sandals on his feet. And get the fatted calf and kill it, and let us eat and celebrate; for this son of mine was dead and is alive again; he was lost and is found!' And they began to celebrate." (Luke 15:11–24)

I am always struck when I reread the parable of the merciful Father; it impresses me because it always gives me great hope. Think of that younger son who was in the Father's house, who was loved; and yet he wants his part of the inheritance; he goes off, spends everything, hits rock bottom, where he could not be more distant from the Father, yet when he is at his lowest, he misses the warmth of the Father's house and he goes back. And the Father? Had he forgotten the son? No, never. He is there, he sees the son from afar, he was waiting for him every hour of every day, the son was always in his father's heart, even though he had left him, even though he had squandered his whole inheritance, his freedom. The Father, with patience, love, hope, and mercy, had never for a second stopped thinking about him, and as soon as he sees him still far off, he runs out to meet him and embraces him with tenderness, the tenderness of God, without a word of reproach: he has returned! And that is the joy of the Father. In that embrace for his son is all this joy: he has returned! God is always waiting for us, he never grows tired. Jesus shows us this merciful patience of God so that we can regain confidence, hope—always! ✠Pope Francis[27]

One of the Pharisees asked Jesus to eat with him, and he went into the Pharisee's house and took his place at the table. And a woman in the city, who was a sinner, having learned that he was eating in the Pharisee's house, brought an alabaster jar of ointment. She stood behind him at his feet, weeping, and began to bathe his feet with her tears and to dry them with her hair. Then she continued kissing his feet and anointing them with the ointment. Now when the Pharisee who had invited him saw it, he said to himself, "If this man were a prophet, he would have known who and what kind of woman this is who is touching him—that she is a sinner." Jesus spoke up and said to him, "Simon, I have something to say to you." "Teacher," he replied, "Speak." "A certain creditor had two debtors; one owed five hundred denarii, and the other fifty. When they could not pay, he canceled the debts for both of them. Now which of them will love him more?" Simon answered, "I suppose the one for whom he canceled the greater debt." And Jesus said to him, "You have judged rightly." Then turning toward the woman, he said to Simon, "Do you see this woman? I entered your house; you gave me no water for my feet, but she has bathed my feet with her tears and dried them with her hair. You gave me no kiss, but from the time I came in she has not

stopped kissing my feet. You did not anoint my head with oil, but she has anointed my feet with ointment. Therefore, I tell you, her sins, which were many, have been forgiven; hence she has shown great love. But the one to whom little is forgiven, loves little." Then he said to her, "Your sins are forgiven." But those who were at the table with him began to say among themselves, "Who is this who even forgives sins?" And he said to the woman, "Your faith has saved you; go in peace." (Luke 7:36–50)

Jesus is the incarnation of the Living God, the one who brings life amid so many deeds of death, amid sin, selfishness, and self-absorption. Jesus accepts, loves, uplifts, encourages, forgives, restores the ability to walk, gives back life. Throughout the Gospels we see how Jesus by his words and actions brings the transforming life of God. This was the experience of the woman who anointed the feet of the Lord with ointment: she felt understood, loved, and she responded by a gesture of love: she let herself be touched by God's mercy, she obtained forgiveness and she started a new life. ✠Pope Francis[28]

In his mercy, God holds the possibility of salvation open for every human being who is fundamentally willing to be converted and who is sorry for his or her guilt, even if their guilt is ever so great and their former life ever so botched up. ✠Walter Cardinal Kasper[29]

When faced with the gravity of sin, God responds with the fullness of mercy. Mercy will always be greater than any sin, and no one can place limits on the love of God who is ever ready to forgive. ✦Pope Francis[30]

I was like a stone lying in the deep mire; and he that is mighty came, and in his mercy lifted me up, and verily raised me aloft and placed me on the top of a wall. —St. Patrick[31]

In his mercy, he never tires of stretching out his hand to lift us up, to encourage us to continue our journey, to come back and tell him of our weakness, so that he can grant us his strength. ✦Pope Francis[32]

When the devil succeeds in frightening us with thoughts of our weakness and frailty, we should not lose confidence; rather we should increase our hope of receiving all the strength we need from God who is all powerful and encourages us to have confidence. —St. Alphonsus Liguori[33]

There has been in history the temptation for some to say: the Church is only the Church of the pure, the perfectly consistent, and expels all the rest. This is not true! This is heresy! The Church, that is holy, does not reject sinners; she does not reject us all; she does not reject because she calls everyone, welcomes them, is open even to those furthest from her, she calls everyone to allow themselves to be enfolded by the mercy, the tenderness, and the forgiveness of the Father, who offers everyone the possibility of meeting him, of journeying toward sanctity.

"Well! Father, I am a sinner, I have tremendous sins, how can I possibly feel part of the Church?" Dear brother, dear sister, this is exactly what the Lord wants, that you say to him: "Lord, here I am, with my sins." Is one of you here without sin? Anyone? No one, not one of us. We all carry our sins with us. But the Lord wants to hear us say to him: "Forgive me, help me to walk, change my heart!" And the Lord can change your heart.

In the Church, the God we encounter is not a merciless judge, but like the Father in the Gospel parable. You may be like the son who left home, who sank to the depths, farthest from the Gospel. When you have the strength to say: I want to come home, you will find the door open. God will come to meet you because he is always waiting for you, God is always waiting for you, God embraces you, kisses you, and celebrates. That is how the Lord is, that is how the tenderness of our Heavenly Father is. ☩Pope Francis[34]

First, the fact that the forgiveness of our sins is not something we can give ourselves. I cannot say: I forgive my sins. Forgiveness is asked for, is asked of another, and in Confession we ask for forgiveness from Jesus. Forgiveness is not the fruit of our own efforts but rather a gift, it is a gift of the Holy Spirit who fills us with the wellspring of mercy and of grace that flows unceasingly from the open heart of the Crucified and Risen Christ.

That is why it is not enough to ask the Lord for forgiveness in one's own mind and heart, but why instead it is necessary humbly and trustingly to confess one's sins to a minister of the Church. In the celebration of this Sacrament, the priest represents not only God but also the whole community, who sees itself in the weakness of each of its members, who listens and is moved by his repentance, and who is reconciled with him, which cheers him up and accompanies him on the path of conversion and human and Christian growth. One might say: I confess only to God. Yes, you can say to God "forgive me" and say your sins, but our sins are also committed against the brethren, and against the Church. That is why it is necessary to ask pardon of the Church, and of the brethren in the person of the priest. ✝Pope Francis[35]

"Very truly, I tell you, anyone who does not enter the sheepfold by the gate but climbs in by another way is a thief and a bandit. The one who enters by the gate is the shepherd of the sheep. The gatekeeper opens the gate for him, and the sheep hear his voice. He calls his own sheep by name and leads them out. When he has brought out all his own, he goes ahead of them, and the sheep follow him because they know his voice. They will not follow a stranger, but they will run from him because they do not know the voice of strangers." Jesus used this figure of speech with them, but they did not understand what he was saying to them.

So again Jesus said to them, "Very truly, I tell you, I am the gate for the sheep. All who came before me are

*thieves and bandits; but the sheep did not listen to them.
I am the gate. Whoever enters by me will be saved, and
will come in and go out and find pasture. The thief comes
only to steal and kill and destroy. I came that they may
have life, and have it abundantly." (John 10:1–10)*

The image of the door recurs in the Gospel on various occasions and calls to mind the door of the house, of the home, where we find safety, love, and warmth. Jesus tell us that there is a door which gives us access to God's family, to the warmth of God's house, of communion with him. This door is Jesus himself. He is the door. He is the entrance to salvation. He leads us to the Father and the door that is Jesus is never closed. This door is never closed; it is always open and to all, without distinction, without exclusion, without privileges. Because, you know, Jesus does not exclude anyone. Some of you, perhaps, might say to me: "But, Father, I am certainly excluded because I am a great sinner: I have done terrible things, I have done lots, of them in my life." No, you are not excluded! Precisely for this reason you are the favorite, because Jesus prefers sinners, always, in order to forgive them, to love them. Jesus is waiting for you to embrace you, to pardon you. Do not be afraid: he is waiting for you. Take heart, have the courage to enter through his door. Everyone is invited to cross the threshold of this door, to cross the threshold of faith, to enter into his life and to make him enter our life, so that he may transform it, renew it, and give it full and enduring joy. ✢Pope Francis[36]

Dear friends, celebrating the Sacrament of Reconciliation means being enfolded in a warm embrace: it is the embrace of the Father's infinite mercy. Let us recall that beautiful, beautiful parable of the son who left his home with the money of his inheritance. He wasted all the money and then, when he had nothing left, he decided to return home, not as a son but as a servant. His heart was filled with so much guilt and shame. The surprise came when he began to speak, to ask for forgiveness, his father did not let him speak, he embraced him, he kissed him, and he began to make merry. But I am telling you: each time we go to confession, God embraces us. God rejoices! Let us go forward on this road. May God bless you! ✠Pope Francis[37]

In my own life, I have so often seen God's merciful countenance, his patience; I have also seen so many people find the courage to enter the wounds of Jesus by saying to him: Lord, I am here, accept my poverty, hide my sin in your wounds, wash it away with your blood. And I have always seen that God did just this—he accepted them, consoled them, cleansed them, loved them. ✠Pope Francis[38]

The LORD is gracious and merciful,
slow to anger and abounding in steadfast love.
The LORD is good to all,
and his compassion is over all that he has made.

The LORD is faithful in all his words,
and gracious in all his deeds.
The LORD upholds all who are falling,
and raises up all who are bowed down.
The eyes of all look to you,

and you give them their food in due season.
You open your hand,
satisfying the desire of every living thing.
The LORD *is just in all his ways,*
and kind in all his doings.
The LORD *is near to all who call on him,*
to all who call on him in truth.
He fulfills the desire of all who fear him;
he also hears their cry, and saves them.

Psalm 145:8–9, 13–19

If the greatest sinner on earth should repent at the moment of death, and draw his last breath in an act of love, neither the many graces he has abused, nor the many sins he has committed would stand in his way. Our Lord would receive him into his mercy. —St. Thérèse of Lisieux[39]

O eternal Mercy, you who cover over your creature's faults! It does not surprise me that you say of those who leave deadly sin behind and return to you: "I will not remember that you had ever offended me." —St. Catherine of Siena[40]

I recommend this prayer to you above all else. When you can say nothing else, simply say, "Lord, help me and help me without delay." —St. Alphonsus Ligouri[41]

PREPARATION FOR TWENTY-FOUR HOURS FOR THE LORD: REFLECTIONS FOR CONFESSORS

The heart of a priest is a heart capable of being moved by compassion, not through sentimentalism or mere emotion, but through the "bowels of mercy" of the Lord! If it is true that tradition points us to the dual role of physician and judge for confessors, let us never forget how the physician is called to heal and how the judge is called to absolve.

But mercy is the heart of the Gospel! Do not forget this: mercy is the heart of the Gospel! It is the good news that God loves us, that he always loves the sinner, and with this love he attracts him to himself and invites him to conversion. Let us not forget that the faithful often find it difficult to approach this Sacrament, both for practical reasons and for the natural reticence in confessing their sins to another man. For this reason it is essential to prepare ourselves, our humanity, in order never to be an obstacle, but rather always to foster their drawing near to mercy and forgiveness. ✝Pope Francis[42]

Let us ask ourselves what mercy means for a priest, allow me to say for us priests. For us, for all of us! Priests are moved to compassion before the sheep, like Jesus, when he saw the people harassed and helpless, like sheep without a shepherd. Jesus has the "bowels" of God, Isaiah speaks about it very much: he is full of tenderness for the people, especially for those who are excluded, that is, for sinners, for the sick who no one takes care of....Thus, in the image of the Good Shepherd, the priest is a man of mercy and compassion, close to his people and a servant to all. This is a pastoral criterion I would like to emphasize strongly: closeness.

Closeness and service, but closeness, nearness!...Whoever is wounded in life, in whatever way, can find in him attention and a sympathetic ear....The priest reveals a heart especially in administering the Sacrament of Reconciliation; he reveals it by his whole attitude, by the manner in which he welcomes, listens, counsels, and absolves....But this comes from how he experiences the Sacrament firsthand, from how he allows himself to be embraced by God the Father in Confession and remains in this embrace....If one experiences this in one's own regard, in his own heart, he can also give it to others in his ministry. And I leave you with the question: How do I confess? Do I allow myself to be embraced? It is a beautiful prayer of mercy! If one experiences this in his own regard in Confession, in his own heart, he is able to give it to others. ✢Pope Francis[43]

Let us return to the Sacrament of Reconciliation. It often happens that we priests hear our faithful telling us they have encountered a very "strict" priest in the confessional, or very "generous," i.e., a *rigorist* or a *laxist*. And this is not good. It is normal that there be differences in the style of confessors, but these differences cannot regard the essential, that is, sound moral doctrine and mercy. Neither the laxist nor the rigorist bears witness to Jesus Christ, for neither the one nor the other takes care of the person he encounters. The rigorist washes his hands of them: in fact, he nails the person to the law, understood in a cold and rigid way; and the laxist also washes his hands of them: he is only apparently merciful, but in reality he does not take seriously the problems of that conscience, by minimizing the sin. True mercy *takes the person into one's care*, listens to him attentively, approaches the situation with respect and truth, and accompanies him on the journey of reconciliation.

And this is demanding, yes, certainly. The truly merciful priest behaves like the Good Samaritan…but why does he do it? Because his heart is capable of having compassion, it is the heart of Christ! ✝Pope Francis[44]

No mother could snatch her child from a burning building more swiftly than God is constrained to succor a penitent soul, even though it should have committed every sin in the world a thousand times over. —Blessed Henry Suso[45]

I will never tire of insisting that confessors be authentic signs of the Father's mercy.

We do not become good confessors automatically. We become good confessors when, above all, we allow ourselves to be penitents in search of his mercy. Let us never forget that to be confessors means to participate in the very mission of Jesus to be a concrete sign of the constancy of divine love that pardons and saves. We priests have received the gift of the Holy Spirit for the forgiveness of sins, and we are responsible for this. None of us wields power over this Sacrament; rather, we are faithful servants of God's mercy through it. Every confessor must accept the faithful as the father in the parable of the prodigal son: a father who runs out to meet his son despite the fact that he has squandered away his inheritance. Confessors are called to embrace the repentant son who comes back home and to express the joy of having him back again.

May confessors not ask useless questions, but like the father in the parable, interrupt the speech prepared ahead of time by the prodigal son, so that confessors will learn to accept the plea for help and mercy pouring from the heart of every penitent. In short, confessors are called to be a sign of the primacy of mercy always, everywhere, and in every situation, no matter what. ✝Pope Francis[46]

And here I want to pause to ask you, for the love of Jesus Christ: never tire of being merciful! Please! Have the ability to forgive that the Lord had, who came not to condemn but to forgive! Be greatly merciful! And if you have scruples about being too "*forgiving*," think of that holy priest about whom I have told you, who went before the Tabernacle and said: "Lord, pardon me if I have forgiven too much, but it is you who have set me a bad example!" And I tell you, truly: it grieves me when I come across people who no longer confess because they have been beaten and scolded. They have felt as though the church doors were being closed in their faces! Please, do not do this: mercy, mercy! The Good Shepherd enters through the door, and the doors of mercy are the wounds of the Lord: if you do not enter into your ministry through the Lord's wounds, you will not be good shepherds. ✝Pope Francis[47]

Lastly, a final point: *the priest is the instrument for the forgiveness of sins.* God's forgiveness is given to us in the Church, it is transmitted to us by means of the ministry of our brother, the priest; and he too is a man, who, like us in need of mercy, truly becomes the instrument of mercy, bestowing on us the boundless love of God the Father.

Yes, as I said before, God is always listening, but in the Sacrament of Reconciliation he sends a brother to bestow his pardon, the certainty of forgiveness, in the name of the Church.

The service that the priest assumes a ministry, on behalf of God, to forgive sins is very delicate and requires that his heart be at peace, that the priest have peace in his heart; that he not mistreat the faithful, but that he be gentle, benevolent and merciful; that he know how to plant hope in hearts and, above all, that he be aware that the brother or sister who approaches the Sacrament of Reconciliation seeking forgiveness does so just as many people approached Jesus to be healed.

Let us not forget that God never tires of forgiving us; through the ministry of priests he holds us close in a new embrace and regenerates us and allows us to rise again and resume the journey. For this is our life: to rise again continuously and to resume our journey. ✠Pope Francis[48]

MARCH 4–5, 2016: JUBILEE CELEBRATION OF TWENTY-FOUR HOURS FOR THE LORD

Acts of Contrition:

- Oh God be merciful to me a sinner!
- My God I am sorry for my sins with all my heart. In choosing to do wrong and failing to do good, I have sinned against you whom I should love above all things. I firmly intend with your help, to do penance, to sin no more, and to avoid whatever leads me to sin.
- I confess to almighty God and to you father, that I have sinned through my own fault, in my thoughts and in my words, in what I have done and what I have failed to do; and I ask blessed Mary, every virgin, all the angels and saints, and you, to pray for me to the Lord our God.

- Oh my God I am heartily sorry for having offended you and I detest all my sins because of your just punishments, but most of all because they offend you, my God, who are all good and deserving of my love. I firmly resolve with the help of your grace to sin no more and to avoid the near occasion of sin.

Prayer of Absolution:

- God the Father of mercies, in the death and resurrection of his son has reconciled the whole world to himself and sent the Holy Spirit for the forgiveness of our sins. Through the ministry of the Church may God give you pardon and peace. I absolve you of your sins in the name of the Father and of the Son and the Holy Spirit. Go in Peace.

Thanksgiving after Confession:

I love the LORD, because he has heard
my voice and my supplications.
Because he inclined his ear to me,
therefore I will call on him as long as I live.
The snares of death encompassed me;
the pangs of Sheol laid hold on me;
I suffered distress and anguish.
Then I called on the name of the LORD:
"O LORD, I pray, save my life!"

Gracious is the LORD, and righteous;
our God is merciful.

The LORD protects the simple;
when I was brought low, he saved me.
Return, O my soul, to your rest,
for the LORD has dealt bountifully with you.

For you have delivered my soul from death,
my eyes from tears,
my feet from stumbling.
I walk before the LORD
in the land of the living.
I kept my faith, even when I said,
"I am greatly afflicted";
I said in my consternation,
"Everyone is a liar."

What shall I return to the LORD
for all his bounty to me?
I will lift up the cup of salvation
and call on the name of the LORD,
I will pay my vows to the LORD
in the presence of all his people.
Precious in the sight of the LORD
is the death of his faithful ones.
O LORD, I am your servant;
I am your servant, the child of your serving girl.
You have loosed my bonds.
I will offer to you a thanksgiving sacrifice
and call on the name of the LORD.
I will pay my vows to the LORD
in the presence of all his people,
in the courts of the house of the LORD,
in your midst, O Jerusalem.
Praise the LORD!

Psalm 116

ON JUDGMENT

He also told this parable to some who trusted in them-
selves that they were righteous and regarded others with
contempt: "Two men went up to the temple to pray, one
a Pharisee and the other a tax collector. The Pharisee,
standing by himself, was praying thus, 'God, I thank you
that I am not like other people: thieves, rogues, adulter-
ers, or even like this tax collector. I fast twice a week; I
give a tenth of all my income.' But the tax collector,
standing far off, would not even look up to heaven, but
was beating his breast and saying, 'God, be merciful to
me, a sinner!' I tell you, this man went down to his home
justified rather than the other; for all who exalt themselves
will be humbled, but all who humble themselves will be
exalted." (Luke 18:9–14)

The Lord asks us above all *not to judge* and *not to condemn.*
If anyone wishes to avoid God's judgment, he should not make
himself the judge of his brother or sister. Human beings, whenever they judge, look no farther than the surface, whereas the
Father looks into the very depths of the soul. ☩Pope Francis[49]

Love of our neighbor consists of three things: to desire the
greater good of everyone; to do what good we can when we can;
to bear, excuse, and hide other's faults. —St. John Vianney[50]

Do not judge, and you will not be judged; do not condemn, and you will not be condemned. Forgive, and you will be forgiven. (Luke 6:37)

Men and women who are merciful have big, big hearts: they always excuse others and think more of their own sins. Were someone to say to them: "but do you see what so and so did?" they respond in mercy saying: "but I have enough to be concerned over with all I have done"…"Who am I to judge this? Who am I to gossip about this? Who am I, who have done the same things, or worse?" ✢Pope Francis[51]

Meekness was the method Jesus used with the apostles. He put up with their ignorance and roughness and even their infidelity. He treated sinners with a kindness and affection that caused some to be shocked, others to be scandalized, and still others to gain hope in God's mercy. Thus he bade us to be gentle and humble of heart. —St. John Bosco[52]

If you are not capable of performing fraternal reproof with love, with charity, in truth and with humility, you will offend, damage that person's heart: you will create an extra tale that wounds and you will become a blind hypocrite, as Jesus says. ✢Pope Francis[53]

Never Condemn. If you want to condemn, condemn your-self. ✠Pope Francis[54]

If you see your neighbor's failing and not your own you will be moved not to mercy but to indignation, not to help him but to judge him, not to instruct him in a spirit of gentleness but to destroy him in a spirit of anger…be gentle, help your brother as if he were sick—as you would wish to be helped in your sickness. —St. Bernard of Clairvaux[55]

If someone is gay and is searching for the Lord and has good will, then who am I to judge him? ✠Pope Francis[56]

Since the goodness of God is so great that one single moment suffices to receive his grace, what assurance can we have that a man who was a sinner yesterday is so today? —St. Francis de Sales[57]

Early in the morning he came again to the temple. All the people came to him and he sat down and began to teach them. The scribes and the Pharisees brought a woman who had been caught in adultery; and making her stand before all of them, they said to him, "Teacher, this woman was caught in the very act of committing adultery. Now in the law Moses commanded us to stone such women. Now

what do you say?" They said this to test him, so that they might have some charge to bring against him. Jesus bent down and wrote with his finger on the ground. When they kept on questioning him, he straightened up and said to them, "Let anyone among you who is without sin be the first to throw a stone at her." And once again he bent down and wrote on the ground. When they heard it, they went away, one by one, beginning with the elders; and Jesus was left alone with the woman standing before him. Jesus straightened up and said to her, "Woman, where are they? Has no one condemned you?" She said, "No one, sir." And Jesus said, "Neither do I condemn you. Go your way, and from now on do not sin again." (John 8:2–11)

Let us ask for mercy…Jesus is clear: be merciful as your Father is merciful…when one learns to blame himself he is merciful with others…and he is able to say: "Who am I to judge him, if I am capable of doing worse things?" This is an important phrase: "Who am I to judge another?" ♱Pope Francis[58]

A person once asked me, in a provocative manner, if I approved of homosexuality. I replied with another question: "Tell me: when God looks at a gay person, does he endorse the existence of this person with love, or reject and condemn this person?" We must always consider the person. Here we enter into the mystery of the human being. In life, God accompanies persons, and we must accompany them, starting from their situation. It is necessary to accompany them with mercy. ♱Pope Francis[59]

Have compassion for me, Lord, help me to feel shame and give me mercy, so that I may be merciful with others. ✠Pope Francis[60]

God is in every person's life. God is in everyone's life. Even if the life of a person has been a disaster, even if it is destroyed by vices, drugs, or anything else—God is in this person's life. You can, you must try to seek God in every human life. Although the life of a person is a land full of thorns and weeds, there is always a space in which the good seed can grow. You have to trust God. ✠Pope Francis[61]

"And you? Who are you? Who are you, who close the door of your heart to a man, to a woman who wants to improve, to rejoin the People of God, because the Holy Spirit has stirred his or her heart?" Thus "they find courage and go." But "how often today in Christian communities" does that man "find the doors closed." Perhaps he hears: "You cannot, no you cannot; you've made mistakes here and you cannot. If you want to come, come to Mass on Sunday, but stop there, don't do anything more."…Even today there are Christians who behave like the doctors of the law and "do the same thing they did with Jesus," by objecting: "This one speaks heresy, this one cannot, this one goes against the discipline of the Church, this one goes against the law." And thus they close the doors to so many people. "Let us ask the Lord today" for "conversion to the mercy of Jesus":

only in this way "will the law be fulfilled, because the law is to love God and neighbor, as ourselves."

I think we too are the people who, on the one hand want to listen to Jesus, but on the other hand, at times, like to find a stick to beat others with, to condemn others. And Jesus has this message for us: mercy. I think—and I say it with humility—that this is the Lord's most powerful message: mercy. It was he himself who said: "I did not come for the righteous." The righteous justify themselves. Go on, then, even if you can do it, I cannot! But they believe they can. "I came for sinners" (Mark 2:17). ✝Pope Francis[62]

The most serious criticism that can be leveled against the church, therefore, is the accusation that oftentimes only a few deeds follow, or appear to follow, its words. The church is reproached for speaking of God's mercy, while it is perceived by many people to be strict, harsh, and pitiless. Such accusations, among others, grow loud with regard to the issue of how the church deals with people whose lives are breaking down or have failed; with civilly divorced individuals who have remarried; with others who have left the church (as is their civil right), often only because they did not want to or could not pay the church tax, or who leave because of the criticism or even rejection of people who lead a way of life that doesn't conform to church order or, in some other way, does not fit into the ecclesial system of rules. ✝Walter Cardinal Kasper[63]

How much harm words do when they are motivated by feelings of jealousy and envy! To speak ill of others puts them in a bad light, undermines their reputation and leaves them prey to the whims of gossip. To refrain from judgment and condemnation means, in a positive sense, to know how to accept the good in every person and to spare him any suffering that might be caused by our partial judgment, our presumption to know everything about him. But this is still not sufficient to express mercy. Jesus asks us also to *forgive* and to *give*. To be instruments of mercy because it was we who first received mercy from God. To be generous with others, knowing that God showers his goodness upon us with immense generosity. ✝Pope Francis[64]

Either you are on the path of love, or you're on the path of hypocrisy. Either you let yourself be loved by the mercy of God, or you do what you want, according to your heart which grows harder, each time, on this path. ✝Pope Francis[65]

In hell there is everything but mercy. That is why God Himself is absent from hell. Mercy is the manifestation of his presence. —Thomas Merton[66]

ON FORGIVING OTHERS

Now his elder son was in the field; and when he came and approached the house, he heard music and dancing. He called one of the slaves and asked what was going on. He replied, "Your brother has come, and your father has killed the fatted calf, because he has got him back safe and sound." Then he became angry and refused to go in. His father came out and began to plead with him. But he answered his father, "Listen! For all these years I have been working like a slave for you, and I have never disobeyed your command; yet you have never given me even a young goat so that I might celebrate with my friends. But when this son of yours came back, who has devoured your property with prostitutes, you killed the fatted calf for him!" Then the father said to him, "Son, you are always with me, and all that is mine is yours. But we had to celebrate and rejoice, because this brother of yours was dead and has come to life; he was lost and has been found." (Luke 15:25–32)

Let us never tire of also going out to the other son who stands outside, incapable of rejoicing, in order to explain to him that his judgment is severe and unjust and meaningless in light of the father's boundless mercy. ✠Pope Francis[67]

Asking forgiveness is not simply making an apology…it isn't easy to receive God's forgiveness: not because He doesn't want to give it to us, but because we close the door by not forgiving others. ✠Pope Francis[68]

The saints had no hatred, no bitterness. They forgave everything. —St. John Vianney[69]

Can there be a Christian who isn't merciful? No. A Christian must necessarily be merciful, because this is the center of the Gospel. And faithful to this teaching, the Church can only repeat the same thing to her children: "Be merciful," as the Father is, and as Jesus was. Mercy. ✝Pope Francis[70]

For this reason the kingdom of heaven may be compared to a king who wished to settle accounts with his slaves. When he began the reckoning, one who owed him ten thousand talents was brought to him; and, as he could not pay, his lord ordered him to be sold, together with his wife and children and all his possessions, and payment to be made. So the slave fell on his knees before him, saying, "Have patience with me, and I will pay you everything." And out of pity for him, the lord of that slave released him and forgave him the debt. But that same slave, as he went out, came upon one of his fellow slaves who owed him a hundred denarii; and seizing him by the throat, he said, "Pay what you owe." Then his fellow slave fell down and pleaded with him, "Have patience with me, and I will pay you." But he refused; then he went and threw him into prison until he would pay the debt. When his fellow slaves saw what had happened, they were greatly distressed, and they went and reported to their lord all that had taken place. Then his lord summoned him and said to him, "You wicked slave! I forgave you all that debt because you pleaded with me. Should you not have had mercy on your fellow slave, as I had mercy on you?" And in anger his lord handed him over to be tortured until he would pay his entire debt. So my heavenly Father will also do to every

one of you, if you do not forgive your brother or sister from your heart. (Matthew 18:23–35)

A Christian, who is incapable of forgiving, sins: he isn't a Christian…if you cannot forgive, neither can you receive God's forgiveness. ✝Pope Francis[71]

Jesus affirms that mercy is not only an action of the Father, it becomes a criterion for ascertaining who his true children are. In short, we are called to show mercy because mercy has first been shown to us. Pardoning offenses becomes the clearest expression of merciful love, and for us Christians it is an imperative from which we cannot excuse ourselves. At times how hard it seems to forgive! And yet pardon is the instrument placed into our fragile hands to attain serenity of heart. To let go of anger, wrath, violence, and revenge are necessary conditions to living joyfully.

Mercy is a key word that indicates God's action toward us. He does not limit himself merely to affirming his love, but makes it visible and tangible. Love, after all, can never be just an abstraction. By its very nature, it indicates something concrete: intentions, attitudes, and behaviors that are shown in daily living. The mercy of God is his loving concern for each one of us. He feels responsible; that is, he desires our well-being and he wants to see us happy, full of joy, and peaceful. This is the path which the merciful love of Christians must also travel. As the Father loves, so do his children. Just as he is merciful, so we are called to be merciful to each other. ✝Pope Francis[72]

LIVING MERCY

Now all the tax collectors and sinners were coming near to listen to him. And the Pharisees and the scribes were grumbling and saying, "This fellow welcomes sinners and eats with them." So he told them this parable: "Which one of you, having a hundred sheep and losing one of them, does not leave the ninety-nine in the wilderness and go after the one that is lost until he finds it? When he has found it, he lays it on his shoulders and rejoices. And when he comes home, he calls together his friends and neighbors, saying to them, 'Rejoice with me, for I have found my sheep that was lost.' Just so, I tell you, there will be more joy in heaven over one sinner who repents than over ninety-nine righteous people who need no repentance.

"Or what woman having ten silver coins, if she loses one of them, does not light a lamp, sweep the house, and search carefully until she finds it? When she has found it, she calls together her friends and neighbors, saying, 'Rejoice with me, for I have found the coin that I had lost.' Just so, I tell you, there is joy in the presence of the angels of God over one sinner who repents." (Luke 15:1–10)

God came out of himself to come among us, he pitched his tent among us to bring to us his mercy that saves and gives hope. Nor must we be satisfied with staying in the pen of the ninety-nine sheep if we want to follow him and to remain with him; we too must "go out" with him to seek the lost sheep, the one that has strayed the furthest. Be sure to remember: coming out of ourselves, just as Jesus, just as God came out of himself in Jesus and Jesus came out of himself for all of us. ✠Pope Francis[73]

"And who is my neighbor?" Jesus replied, "A man was going down from Jerusalem to Jericho, and fell into the hands of robbers, who stripped him, beat him, and went away, leaving him half dead. Now by chance a priest was going down that road; and when he saw him, he passed by on the other side. So likewise a Levite, when he came to the place and saw him, passed by on the other side. But a Samaritan while traveling came near him; and when he saw him, he was moved with pity. He went to him and bandaged his wounds, having poured oil and wine on them. Then he put him on his own animal, brought him to an inn, and took care of him. The next day he took out two denarii, gave them to the innkeeper, and said, 'Take care of him; and when I come back, I will repay you whatever more you spend.' Which of these three, do you think, was a neighbor to the man who fell into the hands of the robbers?" He said, "The one who showed him mercy." Jesus said to him, "Go and do likewise." (Luke 10:29–37)

Jesus tells this parable as a response to the question: Who then is my neighbor? His answer is: not someone at a distance, but rather the one for whom you become the neighbor; the one whom you tangibly encounter and who needs your help in this particular situation. Jesus doesn't preach love of those farthest away, but love of those nearest. This love is not confined to family bonds, friendship, religious, or ethnic membership. This love is gauged according to the concrete suffering and needy person who meets us on the way. ✠Walter Cardinal Kasper[74]

God thinks like the Samaritan who did not pass by the unfortunate man, pitying him or looking at him from the other side of the road, but helped him without asking for anything in return; without asking whether he was a Jew, a pagan, or a Samaritan, whether he was rich or poor: he asked for nothing. He went to help him: God is like this. God thinks like the shepherd who lays down his life in order to defend and save his sheep. ✠Pope Francis[75]

God always wants mercy and does not condemn it in anyone. He wants heartfelt mercy because he is merciful and can understand well our misery, our difficulties, and also our sins. He gives all of us this merciful heart of his! The Samaritan does precisely this: he really imitates the mercy of God, mercy for those in need. ✠Pope Francis[76]

Blessed be the God and Father of our Lord Jesus Christ, the Father of mercies and the God of all consolation, who consoles us in all our affliction, so that we may be able to console those who are in any affliction with the consolation with which we ourselves are consoled by God. (2 Corinthians 1:3–4)

Every Christian, and especially you and I, is called to be a bearer of this message of hope that gives serenity and joy: God's consolation, his tenderness toward all. But if we first experience the joy of being consoled by him, of being loved by him, then we can bring that joy to others. This is important if our mission is to be fruitful: to feel God's consolation and to pass it on to others!

The Lord is a Father and he says that he will be for us like a mother with her baby, with a mother's tenderness.

People today certainly need words, but most of all they need us to bear witness to the mercy and tenderness of the Lord, which warms the heart, rekindles hope, and attracts people toward the good. What a joy it is to bring God's consolation to others! ☩Pope Francis[77]

Then he said to them all, "If any want to become my followers, let them deny themselves and take up their cross daily and follow me. For those who want to save their life will lose it, and those who lose their life for my sake will save it. What does it profit them if they gain the whole world, but lose or forfeit themselves?" (Luke 9:23–25)

The cross is the certainty of the faithful love which God has for us. A love so great that it enters into our sin and forgives it, enters into our suffering and gives us the strength to bear it. It is a love which enters into death to conquer it and to save us....The cross of Christ invites us also to allow ourselves to be smitten by his love, teaching us always to look upon others with mercy and tenderness, especially those who suffer, who are in need of help. ✝Pope Francis[78]

In order to know this God who is love, we must climb the steps of love for our neighbor, by works of charity, by the acts of mercy that our Lord has taught us. ✝Pope Francis[79]

These men without possessions or power, these strangers on earth, these sinners, these followers of Jesus, have in their life with him *renounced their own dignity*, for they are merciful. As if their own needs and their own distress were not enough, they take upon themselves the distress and humiliation and sin of others. They have an irresistible love for the down-trodden, the sick, the wretched, the wronged, the outcast and all who are tortured with anxiety. They go out and seek all who are enmeshed in the toils of sin and guilt. No distress is too great, no sin too appalling for their pity. If any man falls into disgrace, the merciful will sacrifice their own honor to shield him, and take his shame upon themselves. They will be found consorting with publicans and sinners, careless of the shame they incur thereby. In order that they may be merciful they cast away the most priceless treasure of human life, their personal dignity and honor. For the only honor and dignity they know is their Lord's own mercy, to which alone they owe their very lives. He was not ashamed of his disciples, he became the brother of mankind, and bore their shame unto the death of the cross. That is how Jesus, the crucified, was merciful. His followers owe their lives entirely to that mercy. —Dietrich Bonhoeffer[80]

It is from contemplation, from a strong friendship with the Lord that the capacity is born in us to live and to bring the love of God, his mercy, his tenderness, to others. And also our work with brothers in need, our charitable works of mercy, lead us to the Lord, because it is in the needy brother and sister that we see the Lord himself. ✠Pope Francis[81]

A merciful heart does not mean a weak heart. Anyone who wishes to be merciful must have a strong and steadfast heart, closed to the tempter but open to God. A heart which lets itself be pierced by the Spirit so as to bring love along the roads that lead to our brothers and sisters. And, ultimately, a poor heart, one which realizes its own poverty and gives itself freely for others. ✠Pope Francis[82]

Christians are those who let God clothe them with goodness and mercy, with Christ, so as to become, like Christ, servants of God and others. ✠Pope Francis[83]

All the goods that we have received are to give to others, and thus they increase, as if He were to tell us: "Here is my mercy, my tenderness, my forgiveness: take them and make ample use of them." And what have we done with them? Whom have we "infected" with our faith? How many people have we encouraged with our hope? How much love have we shared with our neighbor? These are questions that will do us good to ask ourselves. Any environment, even the furthest and most impractical, can become a place where our talents can bear fruit. There are no situations or places precluded from the Christian presence and witness. The witness which Jesus asks of us is not closed, but is open, it is in our hands. ✠Pope Francis[84]

Extend mercy towards others, so that there is no one in need whom we meet without helping. For what hope is there for us if God should withdraw his mercy from us? —St. Vincent dePaul[85]

CHURCH OF MERCY

We recall the poignant words of Saint John XXIII when, opening the Council, he indicated the path to follow: "Now the Bride of Christ wishes to use the medicine of mercy rather than taking up arms of severity….The Catholic Church, as she holds high the torch of Catholic truth at this Ecumenical Council, wants to show herself a loving mother to all; patient, kind, moved by compassion and goodness toward her separated children." ✠Pope Francis[86]

The Church is a mother: she has to go out to heal those who are hurting, with mercy. If the Lord never tires of forgiving, we have no other choice than this: first of all, to care for those who are hurting. The Church is a mother, and she must travel this path of mercy. And find a form of mercy for all. When the prodigal son returned home, I don't think his father told him: "You, sit down and listen: what did you do with the money?"

No! He celebrated! Then, perhaps, when the son was ready to speak, he spoke. The Church has to do this, when there is some-one…not only wait for them, but go out and find them! That is what mercy is. ✠Pope Francis[87]

Jesus has no house, because his house is the people, it is we who are his dwelling place, his mission is to open God's doors to all, to be the presence of God's love. ✠Pope Francis[88]

As preachers, we will only reach the hearts of our hearers when we speak of God concretely, in light of people's hardships and woe, and help them to discover the merciful God in their own life story. In this process, it does no good only to be critical of the modern world and contemporary human beings (which we are too). We must attend to the present situation with mercy and say that, above all of the fog and frequent gloominess of our world, the merciful countenance of a Father prevails, who is patient and kind, who knows and loves each individual, and who knows what we need.

When the church attests to the mercy of God, it not only proclaims the deepest truth about God, it also proclaims the deepest truth about us humans. For the deepest truth about God is that God is love, which bestows itself and is always ready to forgive anew.…The deepest truth about human beings is that God in his love has created us in a wonderful fashion, that he has not forsaken us even when we have distanced ourselves from him, and that he has mercifully reestablished us and our dignity in a still-more wonderful way. ✠Walter Cardinal Kasper[89]

The Church's intimacy with Jesus is an itinerant intimacy, it presumes that we step out of ourselves, that we walk and sow again and again, in an ever wider radius. The Lord said, "Let us go to the nearby villages to preach, for this is why I have come." It is vital for the Church not to close in on herself, not to feel satisfied and secure with what she has achieved. If this were to happen the Church would fall ill, ill of an imaginary abundance, of superfluous abundance; in a certain way, she would "get indigestion" and be weakened. We need to go forth from our own communities and be bold enough to go to the existential outskirts that need to feel the closeness of God. He abandons no one, and he always shows his unfailing tenderness and mercy; this, therefore, is what we need to take to all people. ✠Pope Francis[90]

I saw that all compassion to one's fellow Christians, exercised in love, is a mark of Christ's indwelling. —Julian of Norwich

The mission of the Church, herself a pilgrim in the world and the Mother of all, is thus to love Jesus Christ, to adore and love him, particularly in the poorest and most abandoned; among these are certainly migrants and refugees, who are trying to escape difficult living conditions and dangers of every kind.

The Church opens her arms to welcome all people, without distinction or limits, in order to proclaim that "God is love" (1 John 4:8, 16). ✠Pope Francis[91]

The Church without frontiers, Mother to all, spreads throughout the world a culture of acceptance and solidarity, in which no one is seen as useless, out of place, or disposable. When living out this motherhood effectively, the Christian community nourishes, guides and indicates the way, accompanying all with patience, and drawing close to them through prayer and works of mercy.

Solidarity with migrants and refugees must be accompanied by the courage and creativity necessary to develop, on a worldwide level, a more just and equitable financial and economic order, as well as an increasing commitment to peace, the indispensable condition for all authentic progress. ✝Pope Francis[92]

This is the Church's mission: healing the wounds of the heart, opening doors, liberating, and saying that God is good, that God forgives all, that God is Father, that God is gentle, that God always waits for us. ✝Pope Francis[93]

Where does Jesus send us? There are no borders, no limits: he sends us to everyone. The Gospel is for everyone, not just for some. It is not only for those who seem closer to us, more receptive, more welcoming. It is for everyone. Do not be afraid to go and to bring Christ into every area of life, to the fringes of society, even to those who seem farthest away, most indifferent. The Lord seeks all, he wants everyone to feel the warmth of his mercy and his love. ✝Pope Francis[94]

Starting from Galilee, Jesus teaches us that no one is excluded from the salvation of God, rather it is from the margins that God prefers to begin, from the least, so as to reach everyone. He teaches us a method, his method, which also expresses the content, which is the Father's mercy. "Each Christian and every community must discern the path that the Lord points out, but all of us are asked to obey his call to go forth from our own comfort zone in order to reach all the 'peripheries' in need of the light of the Gospel" (Apostolic Exhortation, *Evangelii Gaudium*, n. 20). ✢Pope Francis[95]

The Church's mission of evangelization is essentially a proclamation of God's love, mercy, and forgiveness, revealed to us in the life, death, and resurrection of Jesus Christ. ✢Pope Francis[96]

CORPORAL AND SPIRITUAL WORKS OF MERCY

It is my burning desire that, during this Jubilee, the Christian people may reflect on the *corporal and spiritual works of mercy*. It will be a way to reawaken our conscience, too often grown dull in the face of poverty. And let us enter more deeply into the heart of the Gospel where the poor have a special experience of God's mercy. Jesus introduces us to these works of mercy in his preaching so that we can know whether or not we are living as his disciples. Let us rediscover these *corporal works of mercy*: to feed the hungry, give drink to the thirsty, clothe the naked, welcome the stranger, heal the sick, visit the imprisoned, and bury the dead. And let us not forget the *spiritual works of mercy*: to counsel the doubtful, instruct the ignorant, admonish sinners, comfort the afflicted, forgive offenses, bear patiently those who do us ill, and pray for the living and the dead. ✠Pope Francis[97]

Don't get tired of bringing the mercy of the Father to the poor, the sick, the abandoned, the young people and families. Let Jesus be known in the world of politics, business, arts, science, technology, and social media. Let the Holy Spirit renew the creation and bring forth justice and peace in the Philippines and in the great continent of Asia that is close to my heart. ✠Pope Francis[98]

Today too, how many Christians show, not by their words but by lives rooted in a genuine faith, that they are "eyes to the blind" and "feet to the lame"! They are close to the sick in need of constant care and help in washing, dressing, and eating. This service, especially when it is protracted, can become tiring and burdensome. It is relatively easy to help someone for a few days but it is difficult to look after a person for months or even years, in some cases when he or she is no longer capable of expressing gratitude. And yet, what a great path of sanctification this is! In those difficult moments we can rely in a special way on the closeness of the Lord, and we become a special means of support for the Church's mission.

Wisdom of the heart means showing solidarity with our brothers and sisters while not judging them. Charity takes time. Time to care for the sick and time to visit them. Time to be at their side....True charity is a sharing which does not judge, which does not demand the conversion of others; it is free of that false humility which, deep down, seeks praise and is self-satisfied about whatever good it does. ✠Pope Francis[99]

Therefore, a sure path comes by recovering the meaning of Christian charity and fraternal sharing, by caring for the bodily and spiritual wounds of our neighbor. Solidarity in sharing sorrow and infusing hope is a premise and condition for receiving as an inheritance that Kingdom which has been prepared for us. The one who practices mercy does not fear death. And why does he not fear it? Because he looks death in the face in the wounds of his brothers and sisters, and he overcomes it with the love of Jesus Christ. ✠Pope Francis[100]

In the case of the corporal works and especially the spiritual works of mercy, it is interesting to note that we are not dealing with the prohibition of violations of God's explicit commandments. As in Jesus' speech about the Last Judgment, no sinners who murdered, stole, committed adultery, lied, or cheated others are condemned. Jesus' condemnation does not concern violations of God's commandments, but rather failures to do what is good. Again it is a matter of the higher righteousness (Matt 5:20). Accordingly, one can sin not only by violating God's commandments, but also by failing to do what is good, something that, unfortunately, is too-little heeded. ✠Walter Cardinal Kasper[101]

Thus, mercy is concerned with more than justice; it is a matter of attentiveness and sensitivity to the concrete needs we encounter. It is a matter of overcoming the focus on ourselves that makes us deaf and blind to the physical and spiritual needs of others. It is a matter of dissolving the hardening of our hearts to God's call that we hear in the encounter with the adversity of others. ✠Walter Cardinal Kasper[102]

Let us open our eyes and see the misery of the world, the wounds of our brothers and sisters who are denied their dignity, and let us recognize that we are compelled to heed their cry for help! May we reach out to them and support them so they can feel the warmth of our presence, our friendship, and our fraternity! May their cry become our own, and together may we break down the barriers of indifference that too often reign supreme and mask our hypocrisy and egoism! ✠Pope Francis[103]

How many of us, myself included, have lost our bearings; we are no longer attentive to the world in which we live; we don't care; we don't protect what God created for everyone, and we end up unable even to care for one another!

These brothers and sisters of ours were trying to escape difficult situations to find some serenity and peace; they were looking for a better place for themselves and their families, but instead they found death. How often do such people fail to find understanding, fail to find acceptance, fail to find solidarity. And their cry rises up to God!

Today no one in our world feels responsible; we have lost a sense of responsibility for our brothers and sisters. We have fallen into the hypocrisy of the priest and the levite whom Jesus described in the parable of the Good Samaritan: we see our brother half dead on the side of the road, and perhaps we say to ourselves: "poor soul…!" and then go on our way. It's not our responsibility, and with that we feel reassured, assuaged. The culture of comfort, which makes us think only of ourselves, makes us insensitive to the cries of other people, makes us live in soap bubbles which, however lovely, are insubstantial; they offer a fleeting and empty illusion which results in indifference to others; indeed, it even leads to the globalization of indifference. In this globalized world, we have fallen into globalized indifference. We have become used to the suffering of others: it doesn't affect me; it doesn't concern me; it's none of my business!

Lord, we beg forgiveness for our indifference to so many of our brothers and sisters. Father, we ask your pardon for those who are complacent and closed amid comforts which have deadened their hearts; we beg your forgiveness for those who by their decisions on the global level have created situations that lead to these tragedies. Forgive us, Lord! ✝Pope Francis[104]

The easiest to comprehend is physical or economic poverty: no roof over one's head and no food in one's pots, hunger and thirst, or no clothes and no shelter to protect one from the adversities of weather and climate. Nowadays, one would also include unemployment in this list. In addition, there are serious illnesses or disabilities that don't have the opportunity to receive appropriate medical treatment and care.

No less important than physical poverty is cultural poverty: in the extreme case, this means illiteracy; less extreme but still severe is having no chance or reduced chances for education, and, consequently, having slim prospects for the future.

Cultural poverty also includes exclusion from participation in social and cultural life.

The third form of poverty is the lack of relationships. As a social creature, the human person can experience various forms of poverty: loneliness and isolation, the loss of a partner, the loss of family members or friends, communication difficulties, exclusion from social intercourse—whether self-caused or forced upon a person—discrimination and marginalization, including the extreme cases of isolation because of imprisonment or exile.

The final form of poverty to be mentioned is mental or spiritual poverty, which represents a serious problem in the West: lack of orientation, inner emptiness, hopelessness and desolation, despair about the meaning of one's own existence, moral and spiritual aberration to the point of neglecting one's soul. ✝Walter Cardinal Kasper[105]

Christian mercy cannot and may not confine itself to addressing only physical hardships, because mercy is humane only if it doesn't place the needy in an ongoing situation of dependence, but rather provides them with assistance for helping themselves. That is only possible if the cultural, social, and spiritual situation of poverty is also remedied. Christian charity, therefore, makes a holistic approach necessary, which sees the different dimensions of poverty in their reciprocal relations and thus helps to provide not only for mere survival, but rather helps to provide for a life that is at least in some measure humanly fulfilled. ✝Walter Cardinal Kasper[106]

How can I find the wounds of Jesus today? I find them in doing works of mercy, in giving to the body—to the body and to the soul, but I stress the body—of your injured brethren, for they are hungry, thirsty, naked, humiliated, slaves, in prison, in hospital. These are the wounds of Jesus in our day....We must touch the wounds of Jesus, caress them. We must heal the wounds of Jesus with tenderness. We must literally kiss the wounds of Jesus. ✢Pope Francis[107]

We should and we must curb injustice and evil, as far as humanly possible. As far as possible, we must help justice and mercy achieve a breakthrough in society and in the church. Everywhere we can, in situations of physical or spiritual need, we should let the warm rays of mercy shine and thereby ignite a hope-bestowing light of love. ✢Walter Cardinal Kasper[108]

WORKS OF MERCY AND SOCIAL JUSTICE

With regard to the corporal works of mercy, one can perhaps think of the already-mentioned fourfold dimension of poverty, or individual and structural poverty. We can think about the fact that everyday many thousands of people, especially children, die from undernourishment and malnutrition; we can also think of the lack of potable water for millions of human beings. We can also think of migration as a sign of the times and, therefore, also as a challenge of our time: the task of absorbing aliens, who have fallen on hard times at home and seek acceptance from us. In this context, we can think of the task of combating growing xenophobia and hostility toward foreigners. We can think, furthermore, of the problem of the homeless and the street children in many of the large cities of the world. We can easily relate the injunction to visit the sick to the current economizing and concomitant depersonalizing trends in the health care system, or relate the injunction to visit prisoners to the task of humanizing the penal system. ✠Walter Cardinal Kasper[109]

The spiritual works of mercy are equally relevant. The requirement to teach others becomes relevant in light of deficiencies in educational systems or the unavailability of education and training, which is a reason that many fail to have access to social advancement. The injunction to comfort the sorrowful leads to the task of grief counseling; the injunction to counsel the doubtful leads to the task of providing counseling services. Such services are doubly relevant in a situation in which there are hardly any more universally valid standards and many people are overwhelmed by the complexity of modern life. The injunction to admonish the sinner leads, among other things, to raising awareness about unjust structures and disclosing structural injustice. The task patiently to bear what is irksome has a lot to do with tolerance in our pluralistic society. Finally, the exhortation to forgive calls to mind the political meaning of working for peace and reconciliation. ✠Walter Cardinal Kasper[110]

MERCY AND THE POOR

The poor. The poor are at the center of the Gospel, are at the heart of the Gospel, if we take away the poor from the Gospel we can't understand the whole message of Jesus Christ. ✠Pope Francis[111]

What else have you given but from that which you have received from me? You give something earthly; you take something heavenly. You have given from what is mine. I bestow myself upon you. Christ has given himself to you; how can we not also give Christ, who encounters us in those who are in need? Christ gives nourishment and, for your sake, he is in need. He gives and he is needy. If he gives, do you want to receive? If he, however, is in need, do you not want to give to him? Christ is needy when the poor are needy. The one who wishes to bestow eternal life on all has deigned to receive something temporal in the guise of the poor. You want to meet Christ who is enthroned in heaven. Expect to meet him when he lies under the bridges; expect him when he is hungry and shudders from the cold; expect him as the stranger. ✝St. Augustine[112]

The bread that you store up belongs to the hungry; the cloak that lies in your chest belongs to the naked; the gold that you have hidden in the ground belongs to the poor. ✝St. Basil[113]

My daughters remember that when you leave prayer and Holy Mass to serve the poor, you are losing nothing, because serving the poor is going to God and you should see God in them. ✝St. Vincent DePaul[114]

What good is it, my brothers and sisters, if you say you
have faith but do not have works? Can faith save you? If
a brother or sister is naked and lacks daily food, and one

of you says to them, "Go in peace; keep warm and eat your fill," and yet you do not supply their bodily needs, what is the good of that? So faith by itself, if it has no works, is dead. But someone will say, "You have faith and I have works." Show me your faith apart from your works, and I by my works will show you my faith. (James 2:14–18)

We incarnate the duty of hearing the cry of the poor when we are deeply moved by the suffering of others. Let us listen to what God's word teaches us about mercy, and allow that word to resound in the life of the Church. The Gospel tells us: "Blessed are the merciful, because they shall obtain mercy" (Matt 5:7). The apostle James teaches that our mercy to others will vindicate us on the day of God's judgment: "So speak and so act as those who are to be judged under the law of liberty. For judgment is without mercy to one who has shown no mercy, yet mercy triumphs over judgment" (Jas 2:12–13). ✠Pope Francis[115]

My brothers and sisters, do you with your acts of favoritism really believe in our glorious Lord Jesus Christ? For if a person with gold rings and in fine clothes comes into your assembly, and if a poor person in dirty clothes also comes in, and if you take notice of the one wearing the fine clothes and say, "Have a seat here, please," while to the one who is poor you say, "Stand there," or, "Sit at my feet," have you not made distinctions among yourselves, and become judges with evil thoughts? Listen, my beloved brothers and sisters. Has not God chosen the poor in the world to be rich in faith and to be heirs of the

*kingdom that he has promised to those who love him? But
you have dishonored the poor. (James 2:1–6)*

If we are to share our lives with others and generously give
of ourselves, we also have to realize that every person is worthy of
our giving. Not for their physical appearance, their abilities, their
language, their way of thinking, or for any satisfaction that we
might receive, but rather because they are God's handiwork, his
creation. God created that person in his image, and he or she
reflects something of God's glory. Every human being is the object
of God's infinite tenderness, and he himself is present in their
lives. Jesus offered his precious blood on the cross for that person.
Appearances notwithstanding, every person is immensely holy
and deserves our love. Consequently, if I can help at least one person to have a better life, that already justifies the offering of my
life. It is a wonderful thing to be God's faithful people. We
achieve fulfillment when we break down walls and our heart is
filled with faces and names! ✛Pope Francis[116]

MERCY AND THE JUSTICE OF GOD

Mercy is not opposed to justice but rather expresses God's
way of reaching out to the sinner, offering him a new chance to
look at himself, convert, and believe.

If God limited himself to only justice, he would cease to be
God, and would instead be like human beings who ask merely
that the law be respected. God's justice is his mercy given to
everyone as a grace that flows from the death and resurrection
of Jesus Christ. ✛Pope Francis[117]

Mercy is the externally visible and effectively active aspect of the essence of God, who is love (1 John 4:8, 16). Mercy expresses God's essence, which graciously attends to and devotes itself to the world and to humanity in ever new ways in history. In short, mercy expresses God's own goodness and love. It is God's *caritas operativa et effectiva*. Therefore, we must describe mercy as the fundamental attribute of God. ✦Walter Cardinal Kasper[118]

A further grave misunderstanding of mercy occurs if, in the name of mercy, we think we may ignore God's commandment of justice and understand love and mercy, not as fulfilling and sur-passing justice, but rather as undercutting and abrogating it. Therefore, we cannot contravene elementary commandments of justice because of a sentimental misunderstanding of mercy. One cannot advise or provide assistance for an abortion out of a phony sense of mercy, if the birth of a child with disabilities appears to expect too much of the mother or the child. Just as little can one, out of pity for an incurably sick person, offer active assistance in committing suicide in order to "release" him or her from their pain and suffering. Such pseudomercy does not imitate God's mercy; rather, it dismisses God's commandment "Thou shall not murder." ✦Walter Cardinal Kasper[119]

Cheap grace means the justification of the sin and not the sinner....Cheap grace is the preaching of forgiveness without requiring repentance; baptism without church discipline;

communion without acknowledging sin; absolution without personal confession. —Dietrich Bonhoeffer[120]

MERCY AND DIALOGUE

I trust that this Jubilee year celebrating the mercy of God will foster an encounter with these religions (Judaism and Islam) and with other noble religious traditions; may it open us to even more fervent dialogue so that we might know and understand one another better; may it eliminate every form of closed-mindedness and disrespect, and drive out every form of violence and discrimination. ✠Pope Francis[121]

What interests you is to understand the attitude of the Church toward those who do not share faith in Jesus. Above all, you ask if the God of Christians forgives those who do not believe and who do not seek faith. Given the premise, and this is fundamental, that the mercy of God is limitless for those who turn to him with a sincere and contrite heart, the issue for the unbeliever lies in obeying his or her conscience. There is sin, even for those who have no faith, when conscience is not followed. Listening to and obeying conscience means deciding in the face of what is understood to be good or evil. It is on the basis of this choice that the goodness or evil of our actions is determined.

To begin with, I would not speak about "absolute" truths, even for believers, in the sense that absolute is that which is disconnected and bereft of all relationship. Truth, according to the Christian faith, is the love of God for us in Jesus Christ. Therefore, truth is a relationship. ✠Pope Francis[122]

This evening, I ask the Lord that we Christians, and our brothers and sisters of other religions, and every man and woman of good will, cry out forcefully: violence and war are never the way to peace! Let everyone be moved to look into the depths of his or her conscience and listen to that word which says: Leave behind the self-interest that hardens your heart, overcome the indifference that makes your heart insensitive toward others, conquer your deadly reasoning, and open yourself to dialogue and reconciliation. Look upon your brother's sorrow —I think of the children: look upon these…look at the sorrow of your brother, stay your hand and do not add to it, rebuild the harmony that has been shattered; and all this achieved not by conflict but by encounter! May the noise of weapons cease! War always marks the failure of peace, it is always a defeat for humanity. Let the words of Pope Paul VI resound again: "No more one against the other, no more, never!…War never again, never again war!" Peace expresses itself only in peace, a peace which is not separate from the demands of justice but which is fostered by personal sacrifice, clemency, mercy, and love. Let us pray this evening for reconciliation and peace, let us work for reconciliation and peace, and let us all become, in every place, men and women of reconciliation and peace! So may it be. ✝Pope Francis[123]

MERCY AND ECONOMY

A heart troubled by the desire for possessions is a heart full of desire for possessions, but empty of God. That is why Jesus frequently warned the rich, because they greatly risk placing their security in the goods of this world, and security, the final security, is in God. In a heart possessed by wealth, there isn't much room for faith: everything is involved with wealth, there is no room for faith. If, however, one gives God his rightful place, that is first place, then his love leads one to share even one's wealth, to set it at the service of projects of solidarity and development, as so many examples demonstrate, even recent ones, in the history of the Church. And like this God's Providence comes through our service to others, our sharing with others. If each of us accumulates not for ourselves alone but for the service of others, in this case, in this act of solidarity, the Providence of God is made visible. If, however, one accumulates only for oneself, what will happen when one is called by God? No one can take his riches with him, because—as you know—the shroud has no pockets! It is better to share, for we can take with us to Heaven only what we have shared with others. ✝Pope Francis[124]

May the Christians of this nation be a generous force for spiritual renewal at every level of society. May they combat the allure of a materialism that stifles authentic spiritual and cultural values and the spirit of unbridled competition which generates selfishness and strife. May they also reject inhumane economic models which create new forms of poverty and marginalize workers, and the culture of death which devalues the image of God, the God of life, and violates the dignity of every man, woman, and child. ✝Pope Francis[125]

Wash yourselves; make yourselves clean;
remove the evil of your doings
from before my eyes;
cease to do evil,

learn to do good;
seek justice,
rescue the oppressed,
defend the orphan,
plead for the widow.

                                        Isaiah 1:16–17

And those who seek to ease their conscience by attesting: "I'm a serious Catholic, Father, it's really gratifying….I always go to Mass, every Sunday, I take Communion…." The Pope responded: "Okay. But how is your relationship with your employees? Do you pay them under the table? Do you pay them a fair wage? Do you make contributions for their pension? For their health and social security?" Unfortunately, he continued, so many "men and women have faith, but split the Tablets of the Law: 'Yes, I do this'.—'But do you give alms?'—'Yes, I always send a check to the Church.'—'Okay. But at your Church, at your home, with those who depend on you, whether they are your children, your grandparents, your employees, are you generous, are you fair?" Indeed, he stated, you cannot "make offerings to the Church on the shoulders of injustice" perpetrated against your employees. And that is exactly what the Prophet Isaiah sets forth: "One who does not do justice with the people who are dependent on him is not a good Christian." Neither is "one who does not deprive himself of something necessary in order to give it to another who is in need." ✝Pope Francis[126]

To sustain a lifestyle which excludes others, or to sustain enthusiasm for that selfish ideal, a globalization of indifference has developed. Almost without being aware of it, we end up being incapable of feeling compassion at the outcry of the poor, weeping for other people's pain, and feeling a need to help them, as though all this were someone else's responsibility and not our own. The culture of prosperity deadens us; we are thrilled if the market offers us something new to purchase. In the meantime all those lives stunted for lack of opportunity seem a mere spectacle; they fail to move us. ✝Pope Francis[127]

While the Church is called to introduce the leaven and be the salt of the Gospel, that is, the love and mercy of God which reach all men and women, and which point to the heavenly and definitive goal of our destiny, it falls to civil society and political society to articulate and build a life which is more humane, through justice, solidarity, law, and peace. For those who live their Christian faith, this does not mean either fleeing from the world or seeking dominance, but rather it denotes service to the person as a whole and to all peoples, starting with those living on the margins, all the while keeping alive the sense of hope that compels us to work for the good of all, looking to the future. ✝Pope Francis[128]

MERCY AND ECOLOGY

Love for all creation, for its harmony. Saint Francis of Assisi bears witness to the need to *respect all that God has created and as he created it*, without manipulating and destroying creation; rather to help it grow, to become more beautiful and more like what God created it to be. And above all, Saint Francis witnesses to respect for everyone, he testifies that each of us is called to protect our neighbor, that the human person is at the center of creation, at the place where God—our creator—willed that we should be. ✠Pope Francis[129]

We are capable of destroying the earth far better than the Angels. And this is exactly what we are doing, this is what we do: destroy creation, destroy lives, destroy cultures, destroy values, destroy hope. How greatly we need the Lord's strength to seal us with his love and his power to stop this mad race of destruction! Destroying what He has given us, the most beautiful things that He has done for us, so that we may carry them forward, nurture them to bear fruit. ✠Pope Francis[130]

Holy Week and Eastertide

PALM SUNDAY: DIOCESAN DAY FOR YOUTH IN ROME

In the square I have seen that there are many young people here: it is true, isn't it? Are there many young people? Where are they? I ask you who are just setting out on your journey through life: Have you thought about the talents that God has given you? Have you thought of how you can put them at the service of others? Do not bury your talents! Set your stakes on great ideals, the ideals that enlarge the heart, the ideals of service that make your talents fruitful. Life is not given to us to be jealously guarded for ourselves, but is given to us so that we may give it in turn. Dear young people, have a deep spirit! Do not be afraid to dream of great things! ✝Pope Francis[1]

Then they seized him and led him away, bringing him into the high priest's house. But Peter was following at a distance. When they had kindled a fire in the middle of the courtyard and sat down together, Peter sat among them. Then a servant-girl, seeing him in the firelight, stared at him and said, "This man also was with him." But he denied it, saying, "Woman, I do not know him." A little later someone else, on seeing him, said, "You also are one of them." But Peter said, "Man, I am not!" Then about an hour later yet another kept insisting, "Surely this man

also was with him; for he is a Galilean." But Peter said, "Man, I do not know what you are talking about!" At that moment, while he was still speaking, the cock crowed. The Lord turned and looked at Peter. Then Peter remembered the word of the Lord, how he had said to him, "Before the cock crows today, you will deny me three times." And he went out and wept bitterly. (Luke 22:54–62)

Let us also remember Peter: three times he denied Jesus, precisely when he should have been closest to him; and when he hits bottom he meets the gaze of Jesus who patiently, wordlessly, says to him: "Peter, don't be afraid of your weakness, trust in me." Peter understands, he feels the loving gaze of Jesus, and he weeps. How beautiful is this gaze of Jesus—how much tenderness is there! Brothers and sisters, let us never lose trust in the patience and mercy of God! ✠Pope Francis[2]

One of the criminals who were hanged there kept deriding him and saying, "Are you not the Messiah? Save yourself and us!" But the other rebuked him, saying, "Do you not fear God, since you are under the same sentence of condemnation? And we indeed have been condemned justly, for we are getting what we deserve for our deeds, but this man has done nothing wrong." Then he said, "Jesus, remember me when you come into your kingdom." He replied, "Truly I tell you, today you will be with me in Paradise." (Luke 23:39–43)

Today we can all think of our own history, our own journey. Each of us has his or her own history: we think of our mistakes, our sins, our good times, and our bleak times. We would do well, each one of us, on this day, to think about our own personal history, to look at Jesus and to keep telling him, sincerely and quietly: "Remember me, Lord, now that you are in your kingdom! Jesus, remember me, because I want to be good, but I just don't have the strength: I am a sinner, I am a sinner. But remember me, Jesus! You can remember me because you are at the center, you are truly in your kingdom!" How beautiful this is! Let us all do this today, each one of us in his or her own heart, again and again. "Remember me, Lord, you who are at the center, you who are in your kingdom. ✠Pope Francis[3]

Two others also, who were criminals, were led away to be put to death with him. When they came to the place that is called The Skull, they crucified Jesus there with the criminals, one on his right and one on his left. Then Jesus said, "Father, forgive them; for they do not know what they are doing." (Luke 23:32–34)

But the Cross of Christ invites us also to allow ourselves to be smitten by his love, teaching us always to look upon others with mercy and tenderness, especially those who suffer, who are in need of help, who need a word or a concrete action; the Cross invites us to step outside ourselves to meet them and to extend a hand to them. ✠Pope Francis[4]

Mercy courts every human being to the very end; it acti-vates the entire communion of saints on behalf of every individ-ual, while taking human freedom with radical seriousness. Mercy is the good, comforting, uplifting, hope-granting message, on which we can rely in every situation and which we can trust and build upon, both in life and in death. Under the mantle of mercy, there is a place for everyone of good will. It is our refuge, our hope, and our consolation. ✠Walter Cardinal Kasper[5]

Meanwhile, standing near the cross of Jesus were his mother, and his mother's sister, Mary the wife of Clopas, and Mary Magdalene. When Jesus saw his mother and the disciple whom he loved standing beside her, he said to his mother, "Woman, here is your son." Then he said to the disciple, "Here is your mother." And from that hour the disciple took her into his own home. (John 19:25–27)

We are not alone; we have a Mother; we have Jesus, our older brother. We are not alone. And we also have many broth-ers and sisters who, when the disaster struck, came to our assis-tance. We too feel more like brothers and sisters whenever we help one another, whenever we help each other.

Thank you, Lord, for being with us here today. Thank you, Lord, for sharing our sorrows. Thank you, Lord, for giving us hope. Thank you, Lord, for your great mercy. Thank you, Lord, because you wanted to be like one of us. Thank you, Lord, because you keep ever close to us, even when we carry our crosses. Thank you, Lord, for giving us hope. Lord, may no one rob us of hope! Thank you, Lord, because in the darkest moment of your own life, on the cross, you thought of us and you left us a mother, your mother. Thank you Lord for not leaving us orphans! ✝Pope Francis[6]

Jesus, with his Cross, walks with us and takes upon himself our fears, our problems, and our sufferings, even those which are deepest and most painful. With the Cross, Jesus unites himself to the silence of the victims of violence, those who can no longer cry out, especially the innocent and the defenseless; with the Cross, he is united to families in trouble, and those who mourn the tragic loss of their children. We pray for them. On the Cross, Jesus is united with every person who suffers from hunger in a world which, on the other hand, permits itself the luxury of throwing away tons of food every day; on the Cross, Jesus is united to the many mothers and fathers who suffer as they see their children become victims of drug-induced euphoria; on the Cross, Jesus is united with those who are persecuted for their religion, for their beliefs or simply for the color of their skin; on the Cross, Jesus is united with so many young people who have lost faith in political institutions, because they see in them only selfishness and corruption; he unites himself with those young people who have lost faith in the Church, or even in God because of the counter-witness of Christians and ministers of the Gospel. How our inconsistencies make Jesus suffer! The Cross of Christ bears the suffering and the sin of mankind, including our own. Jesus accepts all this with open arms, bearing on his shoulders our crosses and saying to us: "Have courage! You do not carry your cross alone! I carry it with you. I have overcome death and I have come to give you hope, to give you life." ☩Pope Francis[7]

Since, then, we have a great high priest who has passed through the heavens, Jesus, the Son of God, let us hold fast to our confession. For we do not have a high priest who is unable to sympathize with our weaknesses, but we have one who in every respect has been tested as we are, yet without sin. Let us therefore approach the throne of grace with boldness, so that we may receive mercy and find grace to help in time of need....In the days of his flesh, Jesus offered up prayers and supplications, with loud cries and tears, to the one who was able to save him from death, and he was heard because of his reverent submission. (Hebrews 4:14–16, 5:7)

There is no cross, big or small, in our life, which the Lord does not share with us. ☩Pope Francis[8]

He was despised and rejected by others;
a man of suffering and acquainted with infirmity;
and as one from whom others hide their faces
he was despised, and we held him of no account.

Surely he has borne our infirmities
and carried our diseases;
yet we accounted him stricken,

struck down by God, and afflicted.
But he was wounded for our transgressions,
crushed for our iniquities;
upon him was the punishment that made us whole,
and by his bruises we are healed.
All we like sheep have gone astray;
we have all turned to our own way,
and the LORD has laid on him
the iniquity of us all.

When you make his life an offering for sin,
he shall see his offspring, and shall prolong his days;
through him the will of the LORD shall prosper.
Out of his anguish he shall see light;
he shall find satisfaction through his knowledge.
The righteous one, my servant, shall make many righteous,
and he shall bear their iniquities.
Therefore I will allot him a portion with the great,
and he shall divide the spoil with the strong;
because he poured out himself to death,
and was numbered with the transgressors;
yet he bore the sin of many,
and made intercession for the transgressors.
Isaiah 53:3–6, 10–12

Where is your sin? Your sin is there on the Cross. Go and look for it there, in the wounds of the Lord, and your sins shall be healed, your wounds shall be healed, your sins shall be forgiven. God's forgiveness is not a matter of canceling a debt we have with him. God forgives us in the wounds of his Son lifted up on the Cross…the Lord might draw us to himself and that we might allow ourselves to be healed. ✢Pope Francis[9]

I have been crucified with Christ; and it is no longer I who live, but it is Christ who lives in me. And the life I now live in the flesh I live by faith in the Son of God, who loved me and gave himself for me. (Galatians 2:19–20)

God's mercy, which is decisively revealed on the cross, allows us, who have deserved judgment and death, to revive and to live anew, without having earned it. It bestows on us a hope against all hope. It creates a space for life and for human freedom. It neither eliminates human freedom nor suppresses it. On the contrary, this new righteousness restores our freedom anew so that it can be fruitful in works of justice and in our engagement on behalf of justice in the world….In every situation, no matter how hopeless, in life as in death, we are accepted, held, and loved by God.

To believe in the crucified son is to believe that love is present in the world and that it is more powerful than hate and violence, more powerful than all the evil in which human beings are entangled. Believing in this love means believing in mercy. ✢Walter Cardinal Kasper[10]

By your mercy we were created! And by your mercy we were created anew in your Son's blood. It is your mercy that preserves us. —St. Catherine of Siena[11]

After the sabbath, as the first day of the week was dawning, Mary Magdalene and the other Mary went to see the tomb. And suddenly there was a great earthquake; for an angel of the Lord, descending from heaven, came and rolled back the stone and sat on it. His appearance was like lightning, and his clothing white as snow. For fear of him the guards shook and became like dead men. But the angel said to the women, "Do not be afraid; I know that you are looking for Jesus who was crucified. He is not here; for he has been raised, as he said. Come, see the place where he lay. Then go quickly and tell his disciples, 'He has been raised from the dead, and indeed he is going ahead of you to Galilee; there you will see him.' This is my message for you." So they left the tomb quickly with fear and great joy, and ran to tell his disciples. Suddenly Jesus met them and said, "Greetings!" And they came to him, took hold of his feet, and worshiped him. Then Jesus said to them, "Do not be afraid; go and tell my brothers to go to Galilee; there they will see me." (Matthew 28:1–10)

In the life of every Christian, after baptism there is also another "Galilee," *a more existential "Galilee"*: the experience of a *personal encounter with Jesus Christ* who called me to follow him and to share in his mission. In this sense, returning to Galilee means treasuring in my heart the living memory of that call, when Jesus passed my way, gazed at me with mercy and asked me to follow him. To return there means reviving the memory of that moment when his eyes met mine, the moment when he made me realize that he loved me.

Today, tonight, each of us can ask: *What is my Galilee?* I need to remind myself, to go back and remember. *Where is my Galilee?* Do I remember it? Have I forgotten it? Seek and you will find it! There the Lord is waiting for you. Have I gone off on roads and paths which made me forget it? Lord, help me: tell me what my Galilee is; for you know that I want to return there to encounter you and to let myself be embraced by your mercy. Do not be afraid, do not fear, return to Galilee!

The Gospel is very clear: we need to go back there, to see Jesus risen, and to become witnesses of his resurrection. This is not to go back in time; it is not a kind of nostalgia. It is returning to our first love, in order to *receive the fire* which Jesus has kindled in the world and to bring that fire to all people, to the very ends of the earth. Go back to Galilee, without fear! ✢Pope Francis[12]

But on the first day of the week, at early dawn, they came to the tomb, taking the spices that they had prepared. They found the stone rolled away from the tomb, but when they went in, they did not find the body. While they were perplexed about this, suddenly two men in dazzling clothes stood beside them. The women were terrified and bowed their faces to the ground, but the men said to them, "Why do you look for the living among the dead? He is not here, but has risen. Remember how he told you, while he was still in Galilee, that the Son of Man must be handed over to sinners, and be crucified, and on the third day rise again." Then they remembered his words, and returning from the tomb, they told all this to the eleven and to all the rest. Now it was Mary Magdalene, Joanna, Mary the mother of James, and the other women with them who told this to the apostles. But these words seemed

to them an idle tale, and they did not believe them. But Peter got up and ran to the tomb; stooping and looking in, he saw the linen cloths by themselves; then he went home, amazed at what had happened. (Luke 24:1–12)

What a joy it is for me to announce this message: Christ is risen! I would like it to go out to every house and every family, especially where the suffering is greatest, in hospitals, in prisons....Most of all, I would like it to enter every heart, for it is there that God wants to sow this Good News: Jesus is risen, there is hope for you, you are no longer in the power of sin, of evil! Love has triumphed, mercy has been victorious! The mercy of God always triumphs!

Dear brothers and sisters, Christ died and rose once for all, and for everyone, but the power of the Resurrection, this passover from slavery to evil to the freedom of goodness, must be accomplished in every age, in our concrete existence, in our everyday lives. How many deserts, even today, do human beings need to cross! Above all, the desert within, when we have no love for God or neighbor, when we fail to realize that we are guardians of all that the Creator has given us and continues to give us. God's mercy can make even the driest land become a garden, can restore life to dry bones (cf. Ezek 37:1–14).

Let us accept the grace of Christ's Resurrection! Let us be renewed by God's mercy, let us be loved by Jesus, let us enable the power of his love to transform our lives too; and let us become agents of this mercy, channels through which God can water the earth, protect all creation, and make justice and peace flourish. ✝Pope Francis[13]

When I came to you, brothers and sisters, I did not come proclaiming the mystery of God to you in lofty words or wisdom. For I decided to know nothing among you except Jesus Christ, and him crucified. And I came to you in weakness and in fear and in much trembling. My speech and my proclamation were not with plausible words of wisdom, but with a demonstration of the Spirit and of power, so that your faith might rest not on human wisdom but on the power of God. (1 Corinthians 2:1–5)

Believing in the crucified Son means "seeing the Father," means believing that love is present in the world and that this love is more powerful than any kind of evil in which individuals, humanity, or the world are involved. Believing in this love means believing in mercy. For mercy is an indispensable dimension of love; it is as it were love's second name and, at the same time, the specific manner in which love is revealed. ✢St. John Paul II[14]

Blessed be the God and Father of our Lord Jesus Christ! By his great mercy he has given us a new birth into a living hope through the resurrection of Jesus Christ from the dead, and into an inheritance that is imperishable, undefiled, and unfading, kept in heaven for you, who are being protected by the power of God through faith for a salvation ready to be revealed in the last time. (1 Peter 1:3–5)

From the heart of the person renewed in the likeness of God comes good behavior: to speak always the truth and avoid all deceit; not to steal, but rather to share all you have with others, especially those in need; not to give in to anger, resentment, and revenge, but to be meek, magnanimous, and ready to forgive; not to gossip which ruins the good name of people, but to look more at the good side of everyone. It is a matter of clothing oneself in the new man, with these new attitudes.

God is not only at the origin of love, but in Jesus Christ he calls us to imitate his own way of loving: "as I have loved you, that you also love one another" (John 13:34). To the extent to which Christians live this love, they become credible disciples of Christ to the world. Love cannot bear being locked up in itself. By its nature it is open, it spreads and bears fruit, it always kindles new love.

If you go to him with your whole life, even with the many sins, instead of reproaching you, he will rejoice: this is our Father. This you must say, say it to many people, today. Whoever experiences divine mercy, is impelled to be an architect of mercy among the least and the poor. In these "littlest brothers" Jesus awaits us (cf. Matt 25:40); let us receive mercy and let us give mercy! Let us go to the encounter and let us celebrate Easter in the joy of God! ✠Pope Francis[15]

Divine Mercy Sunday Prayer of Sister Faustina

Help me, O Lord, that my eyes may be merciful, so that I may never suspect or judge from appearances, but look for what is beautiful in my neighbors' souls and come to their rescue.
Help me, O Lord, that my ears may be merciful, so that I may give heed to my neighbors' needs and not be indifferent to their pains and moanings.

Help me, O Lord, that my tongue may be merciful, so that I
should never speak negatively of my neighbor, but have a
word of comfort and forgiveness for all.

Help me, O Lord, that my hands may be merciful and filled
with good deeds, so that I may do only good to my
neighbors and take upon myself the more difficult
and toilsome tasks.

Help me, O Lord, that my feet may be merciful, so that I
may hurry to assist my neighbor, overcoming my own
fatigue and weariness. My true rest is in the service of my
neighbor.

Help me, O Lord, that my heart may be merciful so that I
myself may feel all the sufferings of my neighbor. I will
refuse my heart to no one. I will be sincere even with those
who, I know, will abuse my kindness. And I will lock
myself up in the most merciful Heart of Jesus. I will bear
my own suffering in silence. May Your mercy, O Lord,
rest upon me.

You Yourself command me to exercise the three degrees of
mercy. The first: the act of mercy, of whatever kind. The
second: the word of mercy—if I cannot carry out a work
of mercy, I will assist by my words. The third: prayer—if
I cannot show mercy by my deeds or words, I can always
do so by prayer. My prayer reaches out even there where
I cannot reach out physically.

O my Jesus, transform me into Yourself, for You can do all
things.

FIFTH SUNDAY OF EASTER: JUBILEE FOR YOUNG BOYS AND GIRLS (13–16)

Let us think of the meaning of that multitude of young
people who encountered the Risen Christ in Rio de Janeiro and

who bring his love to everyday life, who live it and communicate it. They are not going to end up in the newspapers because they don't perpetrate acts of violence, they don't give rise to scandal and so they don't make news. Yet if they stay united to Jesus they build his Kingdom, they build brotherhood, sharing, works of mercy, they are a powerful force to make the world more just and more beautiful, to transform it!

Are you ready to be this force of love and mercy that is brave enough to want to transform the world? ✝Pope Francis[16]

FEAST OF THE ASCENSION

Then he led them out as far as Bethany, and, lifting up his hands, he blessed them. While he was blessing them, he withdrew from them and was carried up into heaven. (Luke 24:50–51)

Dear brothers and sisters, the Ascension does not point to Jesus' absence, but tells us that he is alive in our midst in a new way. He is no longer in a specific place in the world as he was before the Ascension. He is now in the lordship of God, present in every space and time, close to each one of us. In our life we are never alone: we have this Advocate who awaits us, who defends us. We are never alone: the Crucified and Risen Lord guides us. We have with us a multitude of brothers and sisters who, in silence and concealment, in their family life and at work, in their problems and hardships, in their joys and hopes, live faith daily and together with us bring the world the lordship of God's love, in the Risen Jesus Christ, ascended into Heaven, our own Advocate who pleads for us. Many thanks. ✝Pope Francis[17]

FEAST OF PENTECOST

When the day of Pentecost had come, they were all together in one place. And suddenly from heaven there came a sound like the rush of a violent wind, and it filled the entire house where they were sitting. Divided tongues, as of fire, appeared among them, and a tongue rested on each of them. All of them were filled with the Holy Spirit and began to speak in other languages, as the Spirit gave them ability. (Acts of the Apostles 2:1–4)

This is what the Holy Spirit does in our hearts: he makes us feel like children in the arms of our father….Fear of the Lord allows us to be aware that everything comes from grace and that our true strength lies solely in following the Lord Jesus and in allowing the Father to bestow upon us his goodness and his mercy. To open the heart, so that the goodness and mercy of God may come to us. This is what the Holy Spirit does through the gift of fear of the Lord: he opens hearts. The heart opens so that forgiveness, mercy, goodness, and the caress of the Father may come to us, for as children we are infinitely loved. ✠Pope Francis[18]

This is the precious gift that the Holy Spirit brings to our hearts: the very life of God, the life of true children, a relationship of confidence, freedom, and trust in the love and mercy of God. It also gives us a new perception of others, close and far, seen always as brothers and sisters in Jesus to be respected and loved.

The Holy Spirit teaches us to see with the eyes of Christ, to live life as Christ lived, to understand life as Christ understood it. That is why the living water, who is the Holy Spirit, quenches our life, why he tells us that we are loved by God as children, that we can love God as his children and that by his grace we can live as children of God, like Jesus.

What does the Holy Spirit tell us? He says: God loves you. He tells us this. God loves you, God likes you. Do we truly love God and others, as Jesus does? Let us allow ourselves to be guided by the Holy Spirit, let us allow him to speak to our heart and say this to us: God is love, God is waiting for us, God is Father, he loves us as a true father loves, he loves us truly and only the Holy Spirit can tell us this in our hearts. Let us hear the Holy Spirit, let us listen to the Holy Spirit and may we move forward on this path of love, mercy, and forgiveness. Thank you. ✠Pope Francis[19]

Do you not know that you are God's temple and that God's Spirit dwells in you? If anyone destroys God's temple, God will destroy that person. For God's temple is holy, and you are that temple. (1 Corinthians 3:16–17)

The Holy Spirit also speaks to us today through the words of Saint Paul: "You are God's temple....God's temple is holy, and that temple you are" (1 Cor 3:16–17). In this temple, which we are, an existential liturgy is being celebrated: that of goodness, forgiveness, service; in a word, the liturgy of love. This temple of ours is defiled if we neglect our duties toward our neighbor. Whenever the least of our brothers and sisters finds a place in our hearts, it is God himself who finds a place there. When that brother or sister is shut out, it is God himself who is not being welcomed. A heart without love is like a deconsecrated church, a building withdrawn from God's service and given over to another use. ✠Pope Francis[20]

It is a beautiful image which tells us that the Church is like a great orchestra in which there is great variety. We are not all the same and we do not all have to be the same. We are all different, varied, each of us with his own special qualities. And this is the beauty of the Church: everyone brings his own gift, which God has given him, for the sake of enriching others. And between the various components there is diversity; however, it is a diversity that does not enter into conflict and opposition. It is a variety that allows the Holy Spirit to blend it into harmony.

Let us accept others, let us accept that there is a fitting variety, that this person is different, that this person thinks about things in this way or that—that within one and the same faith we can think about things differently—or do we tend to make everything uniform? But uniformity kills life. The life of the Church is variety, and when we want to impose this uniformity on everyone we kill the gifts of the Holy Spirit. ✠Pope Francis[21]

Peace is not something which can be bought or sold; peace is a gift to be sought patiently and to be "crafted" through the actions, great and small, of our everyday lives. The way of peace is strengthened if we realize that we are all of the same stock and members of the one human family; if we never forget that we have the same Father in heaven and that we are all his children, made in his image and likeness.

Let us ask the Holy Spirit *to anoint* our whole being with the oil of his mercy, which heals the injuries caused by mistakes, misunderstandings, and disputes. And let us ask him for the grace *to send* us forth, in humility and meekness, along the demanding but enriching path of seeking peace. ✠Pope Francis[22]

Ordinary Time II

Prayer is the strength of the Christian and of every person who believes. In the weakness and frailty of our lives, we can turn to God with the confidence of children and enter into communion with him. In the face of so many wounds that hurt us and could harden our hearts, we are called to dive into the sea of prayer, which is the sea of God's boundless love, to taste his tenderness. ✠Pope Francis[1]

How many are your mercies, O God—mercies yesterday and today, and at every moment of my life, from before my birth, from before time itself began! I am plunged deep in mercies—I drown in them: they cover me, wrapping me around on every side. —Blessed Charles de Foucauld[2]

The highest work God has ever performed in all creatures is mercy. The most intimate secret work, even what he has worked in the angels, is carried up into mercy, the work of mercy as it is in itself in God. Whatever God works, the first breaking forth is mercy. —Meister Eckhart[3]

FEAST OF CORPUS CHRISTI

The Eucharist is the summit of God's saving action: the Lord Jesus, by becoming bread broken for us, pours upon us all of his mercy and his love, so as to renew our hearts, our lives, and our way of relating with him and with the brethren. ✝Pope Francis[4]

At times someone may ask: "Why must one go to Church, given that those who regularly participate in Holy Mass are still sinners like the others?" We have heard it many times! In reality, the one celebrating the Eucharist doesn't do so because he believes he is or wants to appear better than others, but precisely because he acknowledges that he is always in need of being accepted and reborn by the mercy of God, made flesh in Jesus Christ.

If any one of us does not feel in need of the mercy of God, does not see himself as a sinner, it is better for him not to go to Mass! We go to Mass because we are sinners and we want to receive God's pardon, to participate in the redemption of Jesus, in his forgiveness. ✝Pope Francis[5]

In the Eucharist the Lord makes us walk on his road, that of service, of sharing, of giving; and if it is shared, that little we have, that little we are, becomes riches, for the power of God— which is the power of love—comes down into our poverty to transform it. ✝Pope Francis[6]

This is why, at the beginning of Mass, every time, we are called before the Lord to recognize that we are sinners, expressing through words and gestures sincere repentance of the heart. And we say: "Have mercy on me, Lord. I am a sinner! I confess to Almighty God my sins." And we don't say: "Lord, have mercy on this man who is beside me, or this woman, who are sinners." No! "Have mercy on me!" We are all sinners and in need of the Lord's forgiveness. It is the Holy Spirit who speaks to our spirit and makes us recognize our faults in light of the Word of Jesus. And Jesus himself invites us all, saints and sinners, to his table, gathering us from the crossroads, from diverse situations of life (cf. Matt 22:9–10). And among the conditions in common among those participating in the Eucharistic celebration, two are fundamental in order to go to Mass correctly: we are all sinners and God grants his mercy to all. ✠Pope Francis[7]

SOLEMNITY OF THE SACRED HEART OF JESUS: JUBILEE FOR PRIESTS

But when they came to Jesus and saw that he was already dead, they did not break his legs. Instead, one of the soldiers pierced his side with a spear, and at once blood and water came out. (John 19:33–34)

In the pierced heart of his son, God shows us that he went to extremes in order to bear, through his son's voluntary suffering unto death, the immeasurable suffering of the world, our coldheartedness, and our lack of love, and sought to redeem them. By means of the water and blood streaming from Jesus' pierced heart, we are washed clean in baptism of all the dirt and muck that has accumulated in us and in the world; and in the

Eucharist, we may always quench our thirst for more than the banalities that surround us and, in a figurative sense, satisfy our thirst for more than the "soft drinks" that are offered to us there. Thus with Ignatius of Loyola's prayer Anima Christi, we can say: "Blood of Christ, inebriate me. Water from the side of Christ, wash me." ✝Walter Cardinal Kasper[8]

By looking at Jesus' pierced heart, that in it God's heart beats for this our world. God's heart is the heart of the world, its innermost power, and its complete and entire hope. We are thus able to endure the darkness of Good Friday in the certainty of a new and eternal Easter morning. It is the certainty that nothing, neither life nor death, will be able to separate us from the love of God in Jesus Christ (Rom 8:35–39). ✝Walter Cardinal Kasper[9]

I am the good shepherd. The good shepherd lays down his life for the sheep. The hired hand, who is not the shepherd and does not own the sheep, sees the wolf coming and leaves the sheep and runs away—and the wolf snatches them and scatters them. The hired hand runs away because a hired hand does not care for the sheep. I am the good shepherd. I know my own and my own know me, just as the Father knows me and I know the Father. And I lay down my life for the sheep. (John 10:11–15)

For this reason being Pastors also means being prepared to walk *among* and *behind* the flock; being capable of listening to the silent tale of those who are suffering and of sustaining the steps of those who fear they may not make it; attentive to raising, to reassuring, and to instilling hope. Our faith emerges strengthened from sharing with the lowly. Let us therefore set aside every form of arrogance, to bend down to all whom the Lord has entrusted to our care. Among them let us keep a special, very special, place for our priests. Especially for them may our heart, our hand, and our door stay open in every circumstance. They are the first faithful that we bishops have: our priests. Let us love them! Let us love them with all our heart! They are our sons and our brothers! ✠Pope Francis[10]

Apostolic and pastoral service means, in the literal sense of the word, wearing oneself out and, precisely in such apostolic and pastoral suffering, letting Jesus Christ, his death, and his resurrection become present for others. Apostolic existence happens not only with words, but with and through one's entire existence. ✠Walter Cardinal Kasper[11]

Here I would like to say a special word to the young priests, religious and seminarians among us. I ask you to share the joy and enthusiasm of your love for Christ and the Church with everyone, but especially with your peers. Be present to young people who may be confused and despondent, yet continue to see the Church as their friend on the journey and a source of hope. Be present to those who, living in the midst of a society burdened by poverty and corruption, are broken in spirit, tempted to give up, to leave school and to live on the streets. Proclaim the beauty and truth of the Christian message to a society which is tempted by confusing presentations of sexuality, marriage, and the family. As you know, these realities are increasingly under attack from powerful forces which threaten to disfigure God's plan for creation and betray the very values which have inspired and shaped all that is best in your culture. ✝Pope Francis[12]

The availability of her priests makes the Church a house with open doors, a refuge for sinners, a home for people living on the streets, a place of loving care for the sick, a camp for the young, a classroom for catechizing children about to make their First Communion....Wherever God's people have desires or needs, there is the priest, who knows how to listen (*ob-audire*) and feels a loving mandate from Christ who sends him to relieve that need with mercy or to encourage those good desires with resourceful charity. ✝Pope Francis[13]

XI SUNDAY OF ORDINARY TIME: JUBILEE FOR THOSE WHO ARE ILL AND FOR PERSONS WITH DISABILITIES

Mother Church teaches us to be close to those who are sick. So many saints served Jesus in this manner! And so many simple men and women, every day, practice this work of mercy in a hospital ward, or in a rest home, or in their own home, assisting a sick person. ✝Pope Francis[14]

Dear young people, I ask you to join me in praying for peace. You can do this by offering your daily efforts and struggles to God; in this way your prayer will become particularly precious and effective. I also encourage you to assist, through your generosity and sensitivity, in building a society which is respectful of the vulnerable, the sick, children, and the elderly. Despite your difficulties in life, you are a sign of hope. You have a place in God's heart, you are in my prayers. I am grateful that so many of you are here, and for your warmth, joy, and enthusiasm. Thank you! ✢Pope Francis[15]

Precisely because of their fragility, their limitations, the sick and disabled can become witnesses of the encounter: the encounter with Jesus, which opens them to life and faith, and to encounter others, with the community. Indeed, *only those who recognize their own fragility, their own limitations, can build fraternal and solid relationships* in the Church and in society. ✢Pope Francis[16]

Lord, may I see you today and every day in the person of the sick and, while caring for them, may I serve you.

Even if you hide in the inconspicuous disguise of an irascible, demanding, or intransigent person, may I recognize you and say: "Jesus, my patient, how good it is to serve you."

O Lord, give me these eyes of faith, for then my work will never be monotonous. I will always find joy in bearing the moods and fulfilling the wishes of all the poor people who are suffering.

O my beloved sick, how doubly dear you are to me when you embody Christ; and what an honor it is for me to be able to serve you.

Lord, make me to appreciate the dignity of my high calling and its great responsibility.

Do not permit me ever to prove unworthy of this vocation by falling into hardheartedness, unfriendliness, or impatience.

And then, O God, because you are Jesus Christ, my patient, condescend to be for me too a patient Jesus. Be lenient with my mistakes and look only upon my resolute intention to love you and to serve you in the person of each of these ailing persons. Lord, increase my faith, bless my effort and my work, now and at all times. Amen. —Blessed Mother Teresa[17]

Unfortunately we know only too well: the endurance of suffering can upset life's most stable equilibrium; it can shake the firmest foundations of confidence, and sometimes even leads people to despair of the meaning and value of life. There are struggles that we cannot sustain alone, without the help of divine grace. When speech can no longer find the right words, the need arises for a loving presence: we seek then the closeness not only of those who share the same blood or are linked to us by friendship, but also the closeness of those who are intimately bound to us by faith. Who could be more intimate to us than Christ and his holy Mother, the Immaculate One? More than any others, they are capable of understanding us and grasping how hard we have to fight against evil and suffering. The Letter to the Hebrews says of Christ that he "is not unable to sympathize with our weaknesses; for in every respect he has been tempted as we are" (cf. Heb 4:15). I would like to say, humbly, to those who suffer and to those who struggle and are tempted to turn their backs on life: turn toward Mary! Within the smile of the Virgin lies mysteriously hidden the strength to fight against sickness and for life. With her, equally, is found the grace to accept without fear or bitterness to leave this world at the hour chosen by God. ✠Benedict XVI[18]

A society truly welcomes life when it recognizes that it is also precious in old age, in disability, in serious illness, and even when it is fading; when it teaches that the call to human fulfillment does not exclude suffering; indeed, when it teaches its members to see in the sick and suffering a gift for the entire community, a presence that summons them to solidarity and responsibility. This is the Gospel of life which, through your scientific and professional competence, and sustained by grace, you are called to spread. ✠Pope Francis[19]

XVIII SUNDAY OF ORDINARY TIME: WORLD YOUTH DAY IN KRAKOW

To you young people I especially entrust the task of restoring solidarity to the heart of human culture. Faced with old and new forms of poverty—unemployment, migration, and addictions of various kinds—we have the duty to be alert and thoughtful, avoiding the temptation to remain indifferent. We have to remember all those who feel unloved, who have no hope for the future and who have given up on life out of discouragement, disappointment, or fear. We have to learn to be on the side of the poor, and not just indulge in rhetoric about the poor! Let us go out to meet them, look into their eyes and listen to them. The poor provide us with a concrete opportunity to encounter Christ himself, and to touch his suffering flesh. ✠Pope Francis[20]

Do not be afraid to live out faith! Be witnesses of Christ in your daily environment, with simplicity and courage. Above all may you be able to show those you meet, your peers, the Face of mercy and the love of God who always forgives, encourages, and imbues hope. May you always be attentive to the other, especially to people who are poorer and weaker, living and bearing witness to brotherly love, to counter all forms of selfishness and withdrawal. ✝Pope Francis[21]

You and your friends are filled with the optimism, energy, and good will which are so characteristic of this period of life. Let Christ turn your natural optimism into Christian hope, your energy into moral virtue, your good will into genuine self-sacrificing love! This is the path you are called to take.

In your Christian lives, you will find many occasions that will tempt you, like the disciples in today's Gospel, to push away the stranger, the needy, the poor, and the broken-hearted. It is these people especially who repeat the cry of the woman of the Gospel: "Lord, help me!" The Canaanite woman's plea is the cry of everyone who searches for love, acceptance, and friendship with Christ. It is the cry of so many people in our anonymous cities, the cry of so many of your own contemporaries, and the cry of all those martyrs who even today suffer persecution and death for the name of Jesus: "Lord, help me!" It is often a cry which rises from our own hearts as well: "Lord, help me!" Let us respond, not like those who push away people who make demands on us, as if serving the needy gets in the way of our being close to the Lord. No! We are to be like Christ, who responds to every plea for his help with love, mercy, and compassion. ✝Pope Francis[22]

MEMORIAL OF BLESSED TERESA OF CALCUTTA: JUBILEE FOR WORKERS AND VOLUNTEERS OF MERCY

Jesus wants to use us to be His mercy, His compassion. That is a Missionary of Charity. Carry His love, His peace.

One day a sister did something terrible. I never said a word to her, but I waited…thinking she will come and say sorry. But she did not come, so I went after her—but no response. I found some other reason to go to her. Still no response. I did not know how she could remain in that sinful state. I felt sorry for her, so I understood how Jesus felt when we refused Him. But He is always waiting. God's mercy is greater than our sin. God has created me for greater things because He loves me.

We must remember—we cannot help seeing the faults of our…people and children, but…we must not ever pass judgment on their intentions—the intention only Jesus knows. That is why Jesus is so very kind and full of mercy because He knows what we really mean each time.

God has chosen you, called you—each of you—by name. It is part of His plan, part of His infinite mercy that He has called us all together, each of us with our particular characters and faults. We need each other. —Blessed Mother Teresa[23]

SEPTEMBER 25, 2016, XXVI SUNDAY OF ORDINARY TIME: JUBILEE FOR CATECHISTS

In the Gospel, Jesus welcomes children, he embraces them and blesses them (Mark 10:16). We too need to protect, guide, and encourage our young people, helping them to build a society worthy of their great spiritual and cultural heritage. Specifically, we need to see each child as a gift to be welcomed, cherished, and protected. And we need to care for our young people, not allowing them to be robbed of hope and condemned to life on the streets.

It was a frail child, in need of protection, who brought God's goodness, mercy, and justice into the world. He resisted the dishonesty and corruption which are the legacy of sin, and he triumphed over them by the power of his cross. Now, at the end of my visit to the Philippines, I commend you to him, to Jesus who came among us as a child. May he enable all the beloved people of this country to work together, protecting one another, beginning with your families and communities, in building a world of justice, integrity, and peace. ✢Pope Francis[24]

SUNDAY, OCTOBER 9: MARIAN JUBILEE

Hail Holy Queen, Mother of Mercy, our life, our sweetness, and our hope. To thee do we cry, poor banished children of Eve; To thee do we send up our sighs, mourning and weeping in this valley of tears. Turn then, most gracious advocate, thine eyes of mercy toward us and after this our exile show unto us the blessed fruit of thy womb, Jesus. O clement, O loving, O sweet Virgin Mary!

Along our path, which is often difficult, we are not alone. We are so many, we are a people, and the gaze of Our Lady helps us to look at one another as brothers and sisters. Let us look upon one another in a more fraternal way! Mary teaches us to have that gaze which strives to welcome, to accompany, and to protect. Let us learn to look at one another beneath Mary's maternal gaze! There are people whom we instinctively consider less and who instead are in greater need: the most abandoned, the sick, those who have nothing to live on, those who do not know Jesus, youth who find themselves in difficulty, young people who cannot find work. Let us not be afraid to go out and to look upon our brothers and sisters with Our Lady's gaze. She invites us to be true brothers and sisters. ✠Pope Francis[25]

When we are weary, downcast, beset with cares, let us look to Mary, let us feel her gaze, which speaks to our heart and says: "Courage, my child, I am here to help you!" Our Lady knows us well, she is a Mother, she is familiar with our joys and difficulties, our hopes and disappointments. When we feel the burden of our failings and our sins, let us look to Mary, who speaks to our hearts, saying: "Arise, go to my Son Jesus; in him you will find acceptance, mercy, and new strength for the journey." ✠Pope Francis[26]

Dear brothers and sisters, because we are all members of God's family, we are called to live lives shaped by mercy. The Lord Jesus, our Savior, is the supreme example of this; though innocent, he took our sins upon himself on the cross. To be reconciled is the very essence of our shared identity as followers of Jesus Christ. By turning back to him, accompanied by our most holy Mother, who stood sorrowing at the foot of the cross, let us seek the grace of reconciliation with the entire people of God. The loving intercession of Our Lady of Tender Mercy is an unfailing source of help in the process of our healing. ✠Pope Francis[27]

Mary sums up in herself the greatest mysteries of faith and radiates them outward. In her shines an image of the new, redeemed, and reconciled person and the new, transformed world that can fascinate us in its inimitable beauty and should pull us out of much torpor and indigence. Mary says to us and shows us: the good news of God's mercy in Jesus Christ is the best thing that can ever be said to us and the best thing that we can ever hear. At the same time, it is the most beautiful thing there can be because it can transform us and our world by means of God's glory, expressed in his gracious mercy. This mercy is God's gift and, simultaneously, our task as Christians. We are supposed to enact mercy. We should live it in word and deed and give witness to it. In this way, our often dark and cold world can become somewhat warmer, lighter, more endearing, and more worth living because of a ray of mercy. Mercy is the reflection of God's glory in this world and the epitome of the message of Jesus Christ, which was given to us as a gift and which we are to further bestow on others. ✠Walter Cardinal Kasper[28]

You are on that journey of those women who followed Jesus in the good and in the bad times. Woman possesses this great treasure of being able to give life, of being able to bestow tenderness, of being able to bestow peace and joy. There is only one model for you: Mary, the woman of fidelity, she who did not understand what was happening but who obeyed. She who, when she learned that her cousin was in need, went to her in haste, the Virgin of Readiness. She who fled like a refugee to that foreign land to save the life of her son. She who helped her Son to grow and stayed with him, and when her Son began to preach, she followed him. She who endured all that was happening to that little child, to that growing youth. She who stayed by her Son and told him what was the matter: "Look, they have no wine." She who, at the moment of the Cross, was by him. Woman has an ability to give life and to bestow tenderness that we men do not have. You are women of the Church. Of the Church, or of the Church which is masculine? No, the Church is not a "he," the Church is a "she." The Church is feminine, like Mary. This is your place. To be Church, to form Church, to stay next to Jesus, to bestow tenderness, to journey, to nurture growth. ✝Pope Francis[29]

NOVEMBER 1: SOLEMNITY OF ALL SAINTS IN MEMORIAL OF FAITHFUL DEPARTED

Let us raise this prayer to God:

"God of infinite mercy, we entrust to your immense goodness all those who have left this world for eternity, where you wait for all humanity, redeemed by the precious blood of Christ your Son, who died as a ransom for our sins. Look not, O Lord, on our poverty, our suffering, our human weakness, when we appear before you to be judged for joy or for condemnation. Look upon us with mercy, born of the tenderness of your heart, and help us to walk in the ways of complete purification. Let none of your children be lost in the eternal fire, where there can be no repentance. We entrust to you, O Lord, the souls of our beloved dead, of those who have died without the comfort of the sacraments, or who have not had an opportunity to repent, even at the end of their lives. May none of them be afraid to meet You, after their earthly pilgrimage, but may they always hope to be welcomed in the embrace of your infinite mercy. May our Sister, corporal death find us always vigilant in prayer and filled with the goodness done in the course of our short or long lives. Lord, may no earthly thing ever separate us from You, but may everyone and everything support us with a burning desire to rest peacefully and eternally in You. Amen" (Fr. Antonio Rungi, Passionist, Prayer for the Dead). ☩Pope Francis[30]

FEAST OF ALL SOULS

Purgatory is not a place and certainly not an otherworldly concentration camp for the expiation of punishments. Ultimately, it is the condition that results from encountering our holy God and the fire of his purifying love, which we can only passively endure and through which we become altogether prepared for full communion with God. It is a pure work of mercy and, in this sense, it represents, so to speak, the last chance granted to us. At the same time, it offers the community of the faithful the possibility, in solidarity, to intercede for the deceased before God. ☩Walter Cardinal Kasper[31]

NOVEMBER 6, XXXIII SUNDAY OF ORDINARY TIME: JUBILEE FOR PRISONERS

Mother Church teaches us to be close to those who are in prison. "But no Father, this is dangerous, those are bad people." But each of us is capable....Listen carefully to this: each of us is capable of doing the same thing that that man or that woman in prison did. All of us have the capacity to sin and to do the same, to make mistakes in life. They are no worse than you and me! Mercy overcomes every wall, every barrier, and leads you to always seek the face of the man, of the person. And it is mercy which changes the heart and the life, which can regenerate a person and allow him or her to integrate into society in a new way. ✠Pope Francis[32]

The past must be abandoned to God's mercy, the present to our fidelity, and the future to God's providence. ✠St. Francis de Sales[33]

Conclusion of the
Holy Year of Mercy

NOVEMBER 13, 2016, XXXIII SUNDAY OF ORDINARY TIME: CLOSING OF THE HOLY DOORS IN ROMAN BASILICAS AND IN DIOCESES THROUGHOUT THE WORLD

In this Jubilee Year, let us allow God to surprise us. He never tires of casting open the doors of his heart and of repeating that he loves us and wants to share his love with us. The Church feels the urgent need to proclaim God's mercy. Her life is authentic and credible only when she becomes a convincing herald of mercy. She knows that her primary task, especially at a moment full of great hopes and signs of contradiction, is to introduce everyone to the great mystery of God's mercy by contemplating the face of Christ. The Church is called above all to be a credible witness to mercy, professing it and living it as the core of the revelation of Jesus Christ. ✝Pope Francis[1]

The starting point of salvation is not the confession of the sovereignty of Christ, but rather the imitation of Jesus' works of mercy through which he brought about his kingdom. The one who accomplishes these works shows that he has welcomed Christ's sovereignty, because he has opened his heart to God's charity. In the twilight of life we will be judged on our love for, closeness to, and tenderness toward our brothers and sisters. Upon this will depend our entry into, or exclusion from, the kingdom of God: our belonging to the one side or the other. ✢Pope Francis[2]

NOVEMBER 20: FEAST OF CHRIST THE KING, CLOSING OF THE HOLY DOORS AT ST. PETER'S

Dear brothers and sisters, being the Church, to be the People of God, in accordance with the Father's great design of love, means to be the leaven of God in this humanity of ours. It means to proclaim and to bring the God's salvation to this world of ours, so often led astray, in need of answers that give courage, hope, and new vigor for the journey. May the Church be a place of God's mercy and hope, where all feel welcomed, loved, forgiven, and encouraged to live according to the good life of the Gospel. And to make others feel welcomed, loved, forgiven, and encouraged, the Church must be with doors wide open so that all may enter. And we must go out through these doors and proclaim the Gospel. ✢Pope Francis[3]

Epilogue

God has chosen the path of mercy as the road Christians walk. During this holy year, we have been pilgrims on this road, journeying to the mercy of God. This is not a geographic pilgrimage, there are no mile markers, no fixed destinations, and this side of heaven, there is no end to our travels. This is a pilgrimage of the soul. We make the journey only to remind ourselves what we seek: the mercy of God, which by God's mercy we already possess. We pilgrims make the journey together to encourage ourselves to keep believing in this merciful love, to believe it so deeply that we live it, to believe it so deeply that we bet our life on it, this life and our life hereafter.

Mercy is the path we aspire to walk; only mercy gives us the strength to live a life of mercy, and that same mercy leads to our ultimate destination, the last threshold we shall ever cross:

"See, the home of God is among mortals.
He will dwell with them as their God;
they will be his peoples,
and God himself will be with them;
he will wipe every tear from their eyes.
Death will be no more;
mourning and crying and pain will be no more,
for the first things have passed away."

And the one who was seated on the throne said, "See, I am making all things new.…I am the Alpha and the Omega, the beginning and the end. To the thirsty I will give water as a gift from the spring of the water of life. Those who conquer will inherit these things, and I will be their God and they will be my children." (Revelation 21:3–7)

Mark-David Janus

Notes

INTRODUCTION

1. *Misericordiae Vultus* 12.
2. R. Frost, "The Death of the Hired Man."

CELEBRATING THE JUBILEE YEAR OF MERCY

1. *Misericordiae Vultus* 12.
2. Ibid., 14.
3. *Evangelii Gaudium* 47.

ADVENT

1. Angelus, December 15, 2013.
2. General Audience, March 27, 2013.
3. Discourses, May 19, 2014.
4. Angelus, June 9, 2013.
5. General Audience, December 11, 2013.
6. W. Kasper, *Mercy: The Essence of the Gospel and the Key to Christian Life*, 157–58.
7. Homily, November 23, 2013.
8. Julian of Norwich, *Revelations of Divine Love* (London: Methuen & Co., 1901)
9. General Audience, May 29, 2013.
10. *Catherine of Siena: The Dialogue* (The Classics of Western Spirituality), 55.
11. Homily, November 7, 2013.
12. Kasper, *Mercy*, 43.
13. Homily, June 16, 2013.
14. *Misericordiae Vultus* 1–2.

15. *Meister Eckhart: Teacher and Preacher* (The Classics of Western Spirituality), 254.

16. Angelus, December 8, 2013.

17. Angelus, December 21, 2014.

CHRISTMASTIDE

1. Homily, December 18, 2011.

2. Pope St. John Paul II, Midnight Mass, December 24, 1978.

3. W. Kasper, *Mercy: The Essence of the Gospel and the Key to Christian Life*, 64, 65.

4. Midnight Mass, December 24, 2014.

5. Ibid.

6. From the Mass of Christmas Day.

7. Homily, Midnight Mass, December 24, 2013.

8. Angelus, August 18, 2013.

9. Mass of Christmas Dawn.

10. Message, December 26, 2013.

11. Angelus December 28, 2014.

12. Homily, October 27, 2013.

13. Kasper, *Mercy*, 146.

14. Homily, December 31, 2013.

15. Angelus, January 4, 2015.

16. Homily, January 1, 1979.

17. Angelus, January 1, 2014.

18. Feast of the Holy Family.

19. Angelus, January 6, 2015.

ORDINARY TIME I

1. Meeting with Youth from Argentina, July 25, 2013.

2. Message, January 21, 2014.

3. General Audience, August 27, 2014.

4. *Dives in Misericordia* 7.

5. Ibid., 15.

6. Kasper, *Mercy*, 132–33.

7. Homily, December 15, 2015.

8. Message, October 4, 2014.

9. *Misericordiae Vultus* 16.

10. Discourses, March 6, 2014.

11. Discourses, August 16, 2014.

12. Kasper, *Mercy*, 135.

13. Angelus, February 2, 2014.

14. Angelus, February 2, 2014.

15. Apostolic Letter to All Consecrated People 2.

16. Ibid., 1.

LENT

1. Homily, September 18, 2014.

2. Homily, January 23, 2015.

3. Discourses, August 19, 2013.

4. Message, October 4, 2015.

5. Message, December 26, 2013.

6. Audience, March 5, 2014.

7. Angelus, September 15, 2013.

8. W. Kasper, *Mercy: The Essence of the Gospel and the Key to Christian Life*, 140–41.

9. Audience, March 5, 2014.

10. *Catherine of Siena: The Dialogue*, 276.

11. *Misericordiae Vultus* 19.

12. Ibid., 12.

13. General Audience, September 18, 2013.

14. General Audience, October 2, 2013.

15. Address of Pope Francis to the Roman Curia, Monday, December 22, 2014.

16. Homily, October 22, 2013.

17. General Audience, June 18, 2014.

18. Homily, April 7, 2013.

19. *Misericordiae Vultus* 17.

20. Kasper, *Mercy*, 165–66.

21. Angelus, March 17, 2013.

22. *Catherine of Siena: The Dialogue*, 275.

23. *Alphonsus de Liguori: Selected Writings* (The Classics of Western Spirituality), 103–4.

24. *Catherine of Siena: The Dialogue*, 268.

25. General Audience, May 29, 2013.

26. General Audience, November 13, 2013.

27. Homily, April 7, 2013.

28. Homily, July 16, 2013.

29. Kasper, *Mercy*, 109.

30. *Misericordiae Vultus* 3.

31. *The Latin Writings of St. Patrick*, trans. Newport John Davis White, 155.

32. Homily, October 13, 2013.

33. *Alphonsus de Liguori: Selected Writings*, 97.

34. Audience, October 2, 2013.

35. General Audience, February 19, 2014.

36. Angelus, August 25, 2013.

37. General Audience, February 19, 2014.

38. Homily, April 7, 2013.

39. *The Story of a Soul*, 199.

40. *Catherine of Siena: The Dialogue*, 71.

41. *Alphonsus de Liguori: Selected Writings*, 101.

42. Discourses, March 28, 2014.

43. Discourses, March 6, 2014.

44. Ibid.

45. *Henry Suso: The Exemplar, with Two German Sermons* (The Classics of Western Spirituality), 197.

46. *Misericordiae Vultus* 17.

47. Homily, May 11, 2014.

48. General Audience, November 20, 2013.

49. *Misericordiae Vultus* 14.

50. *The Sermons of the Curé of Ars*, 133.

51. Homily, March 17, 2014.

52. Ronda Chervin, *Quotable Saints*, 112.

53. Homily, September 18, 2014.

54. Homily, December 15, 2015.

55. *Bernard of Clairvaux: Selected Works* (The Classics of Western Spirituality), 111.

56. Discourses, August 19, 2013.

57. *Introduction to the Devout Life*, 111.

58. Homily, May 2, 2015.

59. Discourses, August 19, 2013.

60. Homily, May, 2, 2015.

61. Discourses, August 19, 2013.

62. Homily, March 17, 2013.

63. Kasper, *Mercy*, 169.

64. *Misericordiae Vultus* 14.

65. Homily, March 12, 2015.

66. *News Seeds of Contemplation*, 91.

67. *Misericordiae Vultus* 18.

68. Homily, March 10, 2015.

69. *The Sermons of the Curé of Ars*, 171.

70. General Audience, September 10, 2014.

71. Homily, November 10, 2014.

72. *Misericodiae Vultus* 9.

73. General Audience, March 27, 2013.

74. Kasper, *Mercy*, 70.

75. Audience, March 27, 2013.

76. Homily, March 5, 2014.

77. Homily, July 7, 2013.

78. Message, December 6, 2013.

79. Homily, January 8, 2015.

80. *The Cost of Discipleship*, 111.

81. Angelus, July 21, 2013.

82. Message, October 4, 2014.

83. Ibid.

84. Angelus, November 16, 2014.

85. Chervin, *Quotable Saints*, 121.

86. *Misericordiae Vultus* 4.

87. Discourses, August 19, 2013.

88. General Audience, March 27, 2013.

89. Kasper, *Mercy*, 160–61.

90. Message, November 16, 2013.

91. Message, September 3, 2014.

92. Ibid.

93. Homily, February 5, 2015.

94. Homily, July, 28, 2013.

95. Angelus, January 26, 2014.

96. Homily, October 12, 2014.

97. *Misericordiae Vultus* 15.

98. Message, October 18, 2013.

99. Message, December 3, 2014.

100. General Audience, November 27, 2013.

101. Kasper, *Mercy*, 143.

102. Ibid.

103. *Misericordiae Vultus* 15.

104. Homily, July 8, 2013.

105. Kasper, *Mercy*, 143–44.

106. Ibid., 144.

107. Homily, July 3, 2013.

108. Kasper, *Mercy*, 204.

109. Ibid., 198.

110. Ibid., 199.

111. Homily, January 16, 2015.

112. Augustine, Sermons #38, trans. W. Kasper.

113. Chervin, *Quotable Saints*, 120.

114. Ibid., 204.

115. *Evangelii Gaudium* 193.
116. Ibid.
117. *Misericordiae Vultus* 21.
118. Kasper, *Mercy*, 88.
119. Ibid., 147.
120. *Cost of Discipleship*, 36–37.
121. *Misericodiae Vultus* 23.
122. Letter, September 4, 2013.
123. Homily, September 7, 2013.
124. Angelus, March 2, 2014.
125. Homily, August 15, 2014.
126. Homily, February 20, 2015.
127. *Evangelii Gaudium* 54.
128. Letter, September 4, 2013.
129. Homily, October 4, 2013.
130. Homily, November 1, 2014.

HOLY WEEK AND EASTERTIDE

1. General Audience, April 24, 2013.
2. Homily, August 7, 2013.
3. Homily, November 23, 2013.
4. Discourses, July 26, 2013.
5. W. Kasper, *Mercy: The Essence of the Gospel and the Key to Christian Life*, 111.
6. Homily, January 15, 2015.
7. Discourses, July 26, 2013.
8. Discourses, July 26, 2015.
9. Homily, April 8, 2014.
10. Kasper, *Mercy*, 79, 82.
11. *Catherine of Siena: The Dialogue*, 71.
12. Homily, April 19, 2014.
13. *Urbi et Orbi*, March 31, 2013.
14. *Dives in Misericordia* 7.
15. Homily, March 28, 2014.

16. General Audience, September 4, 2013.

17. General Audience, April 17, 2013.

18. General Audience, June 11, 2014.

19. General Audience, May 8, 2013.

20. Homily, February 23, 2014.

21. General Audience, October 9, 2013.

22. Homily, May 24, 2014.

ORDINARY TIME II

1. Homily, March 5, 2014.

2. Rene Bazin, *Charles de Foucauld: Hermit and Explorer* (New York: Benziger Brothers, 1923).

3. *Meister Eckhart: Teacher and Preacher*, 253.

4. General Audience, February 5, 2014.

5. General Audience, February 12, 2014.

6. Homily, May 30, 2013.

7. Angelus, September 7, 2014.

8. W. Kasper, *Mercy: The Essence of the Gospel and the Key to Christian Life*, 115.

9. Kasper, *Mercy*, 116–17.

10. Homily, May 23, 2013.

11. Kasper, *Mercy*, 151.

12. Homily, January 16, 2015.

13. Homily, April 17, 2014.

14. General Audience, September 10, 2014.

15. Discourses, May 24, 2014.

16. Discourses, March 29, 2014.

17. *Worte der Liebe* (Freiburg, Herder, 1977).

18. Homily, Lourdes, September 15, 2008.

19. Message, February 19, 2014.

20. Message, January 21, 2014.

21. Message, June 21, 2013.

22. Homily, August 17, 2014.

23. *Where There Is Love, There Is God*, ed. Brian Kolodiejchuk (New York: Doubleday Religion, 2010).

24. Message, January 18, 2015.

25. Homily, September 22, 2013.

26. Message, October 12, 2014.

27. Homily, July 7, 2014.

28. Kasper, *Mercy*, 218.

29. Message, April 26, 2014.

30. Angelus, November 2, 2014.

31. Kasper, *Mercy*, 109–10.

32. General Audience, September 10, 2014.

33. *Introduction to the Devout Life*, 62.

CONCLUSION OF THE HOLY YEAR OF MERCY

1. *Misericordiae Vultus* 25.

2. Homily, November 23, 2014.

3. General Audience, June 12, 2013.

Subject and Contributor Index

Abortion, 105

Absolution, Prayer of, 72

Adultery, 76–77, 96

Advent: call of God and, 17–18; family of God and, 12–13; God seeking out lost people, 14; grace of God and, 17; Immaculate Conception and, 17–18; Jesus as incarnation of God and, 15–16; Lady of Guadalupe and, 9–10; love of God and, 7–8; mercy as foundation of Church and, 10–11; mercy of God and, 8–11, 16; opening Holy Doors of St. John Lateran and all cathedrals, 10–18

Alphonsus Ligouri, St., 55, 61, 66

Anger, 47

Anima Christi (prayer), 134

Ash Wednesday, 42–51

Augustine, St., 102

Baptism, 5, 48, 56–57, 105, 133

Basil, St., 102

Beatitudes, 30–32

Benedict XVI, Pope, 19, 138–39

Bernard of Clairvaux, St., 76

Bible: carrying, 29; door imagery in, 63–64; God's moving toward people in, 11–12; Jesus as incarnation in, 15, 60

Blood feuds, 47

Bonhoeffer, Dietrich, 88, 105–6

Bosco, St. John, 75

Calling of St. Matthew, The (Caravaggio painting), 45

Canaanite woman, 140

Catherine of Siena, St., 13, 48, 55–56, 66, 119

Charity: Christian, 96, 99; Church and, 11; creativity of, 41; deeds of, 34, 39, 88–89; of

people and, 100;
homosexuality and,
76–77; hope and, 26,
87; incarnation and, 60;
inclusivity of Church
and, 50, 92; indifference
and, 109–10; Jesus and,
91, 140; joy of God and,
24, 30; judgment and,
75–80; judgment of God
and, 74; justice and,
109; justice of God and,
104; Lady of Guadalupe
and, 9–10; Last
Judgment and, 148–49;
Lent and, 45–46; lepers
and, 36–37; life as
journey and, 29; lost
people and, 14, 97–98;
love and, 23–24,
129–30; love of God
and, 7–8, 21–23, 67,
124; love of Jesus and,
23, 40–41; Marian
Jubilee and, 142–45;
mass attendance and,
132; material posses-
sions and, 107–8;
Matthew and, St., 45;
merciful heart and, 89;
mercy and, 16, 46–47,
49, 55, 68–69, 146–47;
mercy of God and, 8–9,

23, 36–37, 53–54,
61–62, 65, 83, 104;
misery of world and, 97;
mission of Church and,
93–94; New Year's Eve
and, 26; omnipresence
of God and, 78; opening
Holy Doors of St. John
Lateran and all
cathedrals and, 10–18;
opening Holy Door of
St. Peter's Basilica and,
4–5; parable of prodigal
son and, 58–59; peace
and, 26, 30, 107,
129–30; penitents and,
53–65; personal encoun-
ters with Christ and,
120–21; Peter's denial of
Jesus and, 113; poor
and, 94–95, 100–101,
139; prayer and, 40,
131; Prayer for the Dead
and, 145–46; prayer for
Jubilee Year of Mercy
by, 3–4; presence of
God and, 115–17;
priests and, 67–71,
134–36; prisoners and,
101, 146–47; reconcilia-
tion and, 107; refugees
and, 10, 48, 92–93, 100;
relationships and, 31;

56, 92; compassion of, 41; cross of, 87–88, 104, 114–19, 142–43; Crucifixion of, 113–14; forgiveness of, 42, 57–58, 64, 114, 132; Good Samaritan parable and, 85; Gospels and Jesus' incarnation, 15, 60; grace of, 63; as incarnation of God, 15–16, 23, 60; Last Judgment and, 96; Lent and, 45; love of, 15, 23, 38–41; meekness of, 75; mercy of, 88; mercy of God and, 83; Nativity and, 19–22, 28–29; opening oneself to, 30; personal encounter with, 120–21; Peter's denial of, 112–13; Pope Francis and, 91, 140; redemption by, 10; resurrection of, 94, 104, 120–23, 126; salvation and, 19; sick and, 8–9, 52; sinners and, 44–45, 64, 75, 79, 84, 88, 96, 114; Solemnity of Sacred Heart of, 133–36; suffering of, 38; tax collectors and,

44–45, 84; teaching method of, 94; total Christ, 10; widow of Nain and, 8–9, 59–60; woman anointing, 15–16; Word of, 28, 42; works of charity and, 34; wounds of, 100, 133–34

Jewish tradition, 33–34, 35, 106

John Paul II, St. Pope, 19–20, 26–27, 32, 123

John XXIII, St. Pope, 90

Joseph (Jesus' father), 19, 25

Joy of God, 24, 30

Jubilee, Marian, 142–45

Jubilee for Catechists, 141–42

Jubilee for Clergy, Religious, and Lay Faithful, 35–37

Jubilee for Ill People, 136–39

Jubilee for People with Disabilities, 136–39

Jubilee for Priests, 133–36

Jubilee for Prisoners, 146–47

Jubilee for the Roman Curia, 52–53

Jubilee for sick people, 136–39

Jubilee for Workers and Volunteers of Mercy, 141

Jubilee for Young Boys and Girls, 125–26

Scripture Index